The American West on Film
Myth and Reality

Hayden Film Attitudes and Issues Series
RICHARD A. MAYNARD, Series Editor

The American West on Film
Myth and Reality

RICHARD A. MAYNARD

Films Editor and Educational Film Reviewer
Scholastic Teacher Magazine

Formerly, Teacher of Social Studies and Afro-American History
Simon Gratz High School, Philadelphia; Community College of
Philadelphia; Great Lakes Colleges Association, Philadelphia

HAYDEN BOOK COMPANY, INC.
Rochelle Park, New Jersey

Library of Congress Cataloging in Publication Data

Maynard, Richard A   comp.
    The American West on film: myth and reality.

    (His Hayden film attitudes and issues series)
    SUMMARY: Compares the reality of Western history
with its Hollywood treatment in movies.
    "Filmography": p.
    1. Western films—History and criticism.   2. West-
ern stories—History and criticism.   3. The West—
History—1848-1950.   [1. Western films—History and
criticism.   2. Western stories—History and criticism.
3. The West—History]   I. Title.
PN1995.9.W4M34   791.43'7   74-10945
ISBN 0-8104-5895-0

Printed in the United States of America

1	2	3	4	5	6	7	8	9	PRINTING
74	75	76	77	78	79	80	81	82	YEAR

Editor's Introduction: The Cowboy's West, an American Dream?

"American democracy is . . . the outcome of experiences of the American people in dealing with the West."

Frederick Jackson Turner, Historian (1903)

"The Great Plains Drinks the Blood of Christian Men and Is Satisfied."

O. E. Rölvaag, *Giants in the Earth* (Chapter IV)

"Go West young man . . . if you strike off into the broad, free West, and make yourself a farm from Uncle Sam's generous domain, you will crowd nobody, starve nobody, and . . . neither you nor your children need evermore beg of Something to do!"

Horace Greeley, Editor of the *New York Tribune* (1867)

"But hurrah for Lane County [Kansas], the land of the free,
The home of the grasshopper, bedbug and flea,
I'll sing loud her praises and boast of her fame
While starving to death on my government claim."

Popular Pioneer Song (1887)

"He loved the trackless wilds, rolling plains and mountain solitudes of our land . . . and has stood as a barrier between civilization and savagery, risking his own life to save the life of others."

From *Deeds of Daring!: The Story of Buffalo Bill, The Monarch of Bordermen* (a bestseller of 1879)

"I propose that I shall prosecute the war with vindictive earnestness against all hostile Indians, till they are obliterated or beg for mercy."

Colonel George A. Custer (1876)

"I am tired of fighting. Our chiefs are killed. Our old men are dead. Our young men are dying. It is cold and we have no blankets. The little children are freezing . . . Hear me, white chiefs, I am tired . . . I will fight no more . . . forever."

Chief Joseph of the Nez Percé Tribe (1877)

"He is America's Robin Hood. He never fails to distribute his stolen loot among weeping widows about to lose their homesteads. Old men receive his coat in the freezing cold with tearful thanks."

WANTED FOR MURDER AND ROBBERY

JESSE JAMES

DEAD OR ALIVE

$25,000. REWARD

St. Louis Midland Railroad (1876)

"The country needs heroes . . . When the legend becomes a fact . . . show the legend!"

John Ford, Director of over 50 Western films

"The emerging shape of a new world order, and the requisites for survival in such a new world, are fostering in young whites a new outlook. They recoil in shame from the spectacle of cowboys and pioneers—their heroic forefathers whose exploits filled earlier generations with pride—galloping across a movie screen shooting down Indians like Coke bottles."

Eldridge Cleaver, *Soul on Ice* (1968)

"It's life's illusions I recall,
I really don't know life, at all."

Clouds, Popular song (1969)

No figure has dominated American romantic folklore like the legendary cowboy. Daring, noble, ethical, romantic, he permeates our popular media to this very day. He personifies our national self-image—the conqueror of wilderness, savagery, and villainy. He is America's knight-errant with a Colt 45.

Our fascination with this mythical figure and the great plains he is alleged to have conquered has nothing whatsoever to do with the actual history of the American West. The national hero-worship of the Westerner is based on needs within American society which cause us to reproduce the cowboy legend generation after generation through our popular mass media. Western novels and films are engrained traditions of American culture, and we need to understand why they exist and how they help shape our national personality.

The purpose of this anthology and the films that should accompany it is to examine the roots of the Western legend and their implications. It begins by outlining the reality of Western history, which is essentially drab and unromantic. Once the true Western past is understood, the myth which engulfs it is analyzed. Hence the bulk of this volume concentrates on the fabric of the legend itself. It includes extracts from popular Western literature, as well as literary and historical analyses of such material. Most of the data, however, deals with movies. Screenplay extracts, still-photographs from Westerns, promotional copy, contemporary reviews, as well as criticism from leading film scholars, are presented to provide as broad an examination of the Western myth as possible.

Our national preoccupation with the cowboy legend reflects an American tradition of militant individualism, violence, White supremacy, and an often contradictory code of right and wrong. Recent treatments of Western lore tend to have become more humane, but the mystique of the cowboy's West still dominates our culture, demonstrated by the continuing popularity of the Western movie. This work, like others in the *Film Attitudes and Issues* series, is designed to show that an analysis of our mass media—particularly films—can be a useful reflector of American society in general.

Extracts from several of the key films discussed in this unit are available from Films Incorporated in Wilmette, Illinois, on a 30-minute, 16-mm sound film, *The American West on Film: Myth and Reality.*

Contents

The American West on Film
Myth and Reality

PART ONE

The West As Fact

Have you ever noticed that most Western movies take place sometime between the years 1870-1890? The movies tell us (as did the popular Western novels which preceded them) that the peak of the Wild West lasted only about twenty years. Yet, if we are to believe the popular media, these twenty years were crammed with the romantic deeds of the nerves-of-iron gunfighter, the Robin Hood outlaw, the scrupulous lawman, the dashing cavalry officer, and the noble cowboy. This twenty-year period represents probably the most heroic, most romanticized, and—with the unending popularity of Western novels and films—most dramatized period of American history.

Historically speaking, this period was extremely important. 1870-1890 was the era of American industrialization, marking unprecedented progress in the technological development of the nation. It was an era, also, of increasing urbanization and massive foreign immigration. And it was a time of political evil, economic corruption, and vicious racism.

Somehow, however, in spite of the vast complexity of the major events of 1870-1890, American popular culture only chooses to portray and commemorate a very minor occurrence of that period—the conquest of the Western plains.

Before we examine the reasons behind America's fascination with her frontier heritage (and the great mythology which surrounds it), we ought to take a close look at the real West of 1870-1890. The West of the legendary cowboy and gunslinger bears little resemblance to the barren, lonely wilderness of the plains. The "heroes" of the real West were humble farmers and beleaguered cattle drovers. The "villains" of the real West weren't quick-drawing outlaws. They were wind, rain, and cold. They were loneliness and isolation.

The first part of this section includes a few samples of what it was like to live in the real West of 1870-1890—a letter from a Nebraska homesteader; a Texas cattle drover's diary; an excerpt from O. E. Rölvaag's, *Giants in the Earth* (often considered the most realistic novel ever written about life on the plains); and a popular frontier song of 1890. Compare these descriptions to the West you saw most recently in the movies or on television.

THE GUNFIGHTER AND THE OUTLAW

Two of the staple figures of our Western mythology are the gunfighter and the outlaw. The fearless, fast-draw gunman and the romantic, Robin Hood

1

bandit have blazed through countless horse opera novels and movies. Indeed, in many, these two figures were one and the same man.

In the second part of this section we examine the reality behind these legends. The true nature of gunslinger and outlaw is exposed by historian Joseph Rosa as he examines the image of the gunfighter in relationship to the West of the 1870s and 1880s, and questions whether, in fact, he ever existed at all.

from The Letters of Ed Donnell,
A Nebraska Homesteader

[Ed Donnell was a representative homesteader. A bachelor, he came from a poor family in Missouri and took up a claim in Sherman County, Nebraska, in 1884. He worked hard, soon married, lived frugally, and showed a certain restlessness about moving on.]

Basora [Nebraska]

October the/8 [1885]

Dear Mother: . . . Fall is here again. It has been cool for a week or two froze a little last night. I finished digging my potatoes yesterday, had 27 bushels, about a bushel of beats, brought in about a bushel of green tomatoes last eve to make pickleelilly—

You wanted to know how I liked my new home and how I was getting along. I like Nebr first rate wouldnt look at a thousand dollars for my claim, but I have had poor health since July until a couple of weeks ago. I quit working so hard and am getting stout again. I have saw a pretty tuff time a part of the time since I have been out here, but I started out to get a home and I was determined to win or die in the attempt. I worked to hard in the fore part of the season, I would get up early and get my breakfast and get out to work. Scarcely ever set down only while I was eating from the time I got up until I went to bed at nine and ten o'clock.

I will tell you what kind of a house I lived in last winter. It was a sod house of corse, but it was so late when I got it built that I didnt get it plastered until spring. Nothing but the ground for a floor. A bedstead with wilow poles for slats. Boxes to sit on. And if it didnt look pretty rough I dont want to see anything that does. And there was nothing to do all winter so I had to make the best of it. There is lots of other bachelors here but I am the only one I know who doesnt have kinfolks living handy so that they can help in the way of cooking. I had no relatives handy but I think I have as many friends as anybody Aunt Jennie and the girls has always been so good to me. They have baked bread and washed for me part of the time—would all of the time if I would have let them. . . .

From "The Letters of Ed Donnell," edited by Charles J. Wilkerson. **Nebraska History,** XLI (June 1960).

I broke out about 30 acres last spring besides putting in my crop and tending it. Have put between too and three hundred dollars worth of improvements on my place. Have got a good crop of corn,. a floor in my house and got it ceiled overhead and a calico petition, a bedstead and cupboard, some dishes and chairs. I got five hogs. In fact, things look quite different to what they did last fall. Times is dull here now. Wheat is only worth thirty cents a bushel. I worked out some in harvest but havent got no money for it yet. A person borrows money here they have to pay 3 percent per month, the same as 36 percent per year. I had to borrow 20 dollars this summer that thats what I had to pay.

You wanted to know when I was going to get married. Just as quick as I can get money ahead to get a cow and to get married. I want to before I commence shucking corn if I can to Aunt Jennie's oldest girl. She is 18 years old. She is a good girl and knows how to work. We are going to get our pictures taken and send Home. A fellow cant do much good on a new place when he has everything to do both indoors and out both. She says if we marry right away she is going to do the work in the house and shuck the down row when I am gathering corn, but I will be glad enough to get rid of the housework.

You spoke about sending some bedclothes and I believe I will let you send them. I would like to have a featherbed. I have been trying to get feathers, but I cant find a pound at the towns or in the country. I wish you would find out what twenty pounds of feathers would cost and write immediately and let me know. . . . I dont want a word told that is in this letter outside of the family burn it when you read it.

Arcadia [Nebraska]

March 28, [1887]

Dear Brother: . . . We have had a month of pretty weather. People is done sowing wheat. I am going to put all my ground in corn am going to break out a lot more ground this summer. I built me a little frame stable this spring. The rats eat my sod stable down or so that it fell. I may sell out this summer land is going up fast. My place is worth 2000. Wont take any less. If I sell out I am going west and grow up with the country. . . . They are working on the railroad between loop city and arcadia now. We will hear the iron horse a snorting in Arcadia by the 4th of July.

There is not many churches here yet, but I dont think it is any closer to hell than it is any place else for my new well is 125 feet to water and it is almost as cold as ice. I like to have churches and go to them, but I dont think God requires people to stay in a country where they shake their liver upside down or where they cant make a liven or have a home, just because they have churches. For my part, I like to have a little health and something to eat and try to lay up something for a rainy day and old age. Charley, you can do as you please, but if I were you I would make a break for a home as soon as you are old enough to take land. If I had started out to Neb when I was 21 if I hadnt a cent left when I got here I would have been well off now. If you was of age and out here I could get you a claim but it would be rough but there is good land west of here and they say there is plenty of timber. If you want to come west I will help to keep the folks at home.

Arcadia, Valy Co. Nebr.

Sept 1 [1887]

Dear Father and Mother: . . . We have been having wet weather for 3 weeks and is still raining. The drough and chintz bugs hurt the corn but there is a fare crop yet. There will be lots of corn to spare I will have plenty to do me and a little to spare I have 48 head of hogs and they eat a good deal of corn. I am trying to sell out. My health has been so poor this summer and the wind and sun hurts my head so. I think if I sell I will get me a timber claim and move to town for I can get $40 a month working in a grist mill and I would not be exposed to the weather. A person dont have to live on a timber claim or wont have any taxes to pay on it for 8 years. Taxes is unreasonable in this country. My taxes will be about $40 this year. . . .

Diary of George C. Duffield, A Cattle Drover

[no date; around 1880]

March 20th. Struck out to make a trade crossed the Cherokee and stopped for the night at a Mr. Barbers contracted for 1000 Head of Beeves at 12$ p. head.

26th. started at 8 A.M. for Galveston via Buffalo Bayou Brazos Colorado R R Arrived at Richmond for Dinner and to Harrisburg at 2 P M distance 80 Miles. From Alleytown to Richmond on the Brazos River the Road ran through the Most beautiful Prairie that I ever laid eyes on Pasture was abundant and the Prairie was literally covered with tens of thousands of cattle Horses and Mules. . . . From Rich to this place the country is Level good grass and thousands of cattle . . . Left at 3 for Galveston and arrived at 7 P.M Country level. put at Island City Hotel Fare 5$ gold pr day.

April 5th. Started for Sansaba with two wagons and 5 yoke Oxen and Seven hands. Travelled 12 Miles and camped. Rained hard during the night.

15th. Returned to Camp found 4 new hands had come to Camp Making 20 in all. It Rained hard while we were gone and the River rose. great sport and Men wet crossing.

16th. Lay round Camp had two Horse races won two bits on each went in swimming—fishing and had a gay day—all the Fish to eat we want.

From "Driving Cattle from Texas to Iowa, 1866: George C. Duffield's Diary," **Annals of Iowa** (published by the Iowa State Department of History and Archives), Third Series, XIV (April 1924).

21. Rode to Mr. Harrells where Boys were hearding Cattle for Him. slept by cattle pen—cattle stampeded and 150 got away.

23rd. Packed up for off Travelled six Miles to first pen and camped Rode 15 More to Mr. Montgomerys.

24th. back over the mountains to Camp at Harrels Recd 241 cattle and finished Branding Pen hearded *all* night.

27th. finished Branding Started for Salt Creek with 835 Beeves Landed safe.

May 1st. Travelled 10 miles to Corryell co Big Stamped lost 200 head of cattle.

2ond. Spent the day hunting and found but 25 Head it has been Raining for three days these are dark days for me.

3rd. day Spent in hunting cattle found 23 hard rain and wind lots of trouble.

4th. Continued the hunt found 40 head day pleasant. Sun shone once more. Heard that the other Herd has stampeded and lost over 200.

5. Cloudy damp Morning rode 16 Miles and back to see the other Boys found them in trouble with cattle all scattered over the country.

7th. Hunt cattle is the order of the day—found most of our Cattle and drove 12 miles and camped on a large creek in Bosque Co.

8th. All 3 heards are up and ready to travel off together for the first time travelled 6 miles rain pouring down in torrents and here we are on the banks of a creek with 10 or 12 ft water and raising crossed at 4 Oclock and crossed into the Bosque Bottom found it 20 ft deep Ran my Horse into a ditch and got my Knee badly sprained—15 Miles.

9th. Still dark and gloomy River up everything looks *Blue* to me no crossing to day cattle behaved well.

13th. Big Thunder Storm last night Stampede lost 100 Beeves hunted all day found 50 all tired. Every thing discouraging.

14th. Concluded to cross Brazos swam our cattle and Horses and built Raft and Rafted our provisions and blankets &c over Swam River with rope and then hauled wagon over lost Most of our Kitchen furniture such as camp Kittles Coffee Pots Cups Plates Canteens &c &c.

15. back at River bringing up wagon Hunting Oxen and other *lost* property. Rain poured down for one Hour. It does nothing but rain got all our *traps* together that was not lost and thought we were ready for off dark rainy night cattle all left us and in morning not one Beef to be seen.

16th. Hunt Beeves is the word—all Hands discouraged and are determined to go 200 Beeves out and nothing to eat.

18th. Everything gloomey four best hands left us got to Buchanon at noon and to Rock Creek in Johnston Co distance 14 [miles].

20th. Rain poured down for two hours Ground in a flood Creeks up—Hands leaving Gloomey times as ever I saw drove 8 miles with 5 hands (359 Head) passed the night 6 miles S.W. from Fort Worth in Parker Co.

22nd. This day has been spent in crossing the West Trinity and a hard and long to be remembered day for me we swam our cattle and Horses. I swam it 5 times upset our wagon in River and lost Many of our cooking utencils again drove 3 miles and camped.

23rd. Travelled 10 Miles over a beautiful Prairie country such as I expected to see before I came here stopped for dinner on Henrietta Creek and then on to Elisabeth Town and creek and stopped for the night—Hard rain that night and cattle behaved very bad—ran all night—was on my Horse the whole night and it raining hard.

24th. Glad to see Morning come counted and found we had lost none for the first time—feel very bad. travelled 14 miles crossed Denton Creek.

29th. Moved up to River and after many difficulties got all my Drove over but 100.

30th. worked in River all day and 50 Beeves on this side of River yet—am still in Texas.

31st. Swimming Cattle is the order We worked all day in the River and at dusk got the last Beefe over—and am now out of Texas—This day will long be remembered by men—There was one of our party Drowned to day (Mr Carr) and several narrow escapes and I among the no.

June [I]st. Stampede last night among 6 droves and a general mix up and loss of Beeves. Hunt Cattle again Men all tired and want to leave. am in the Indian country am annoyed by them believe they scare the Cattle to get pay to collect them—Spent the day in separating Beeves and Hunting—Two men and Bunch Beeves lost—Many Men in trouble. Horses *all* give out and Men refused to do anything.

2ond. Hard rain and wind Storm Beeves ran and had to be on Horse back all night. Awful night. wet all night clear bright morning. Men still lost quit the Beeves and go to Hunting Men is the word—4 P.M. Found our men with Indian guide and 195 Beeves 14 Miles from camp. almost starved not having had a bite to eat for 60 hours got to camp about 12 M *Tired*

5th. Oh! what a night—Thunder Lightning and rain—we followed our Beeves *all* night as they wandered about—put them on the road at day break found 90 beeves of an other mans Herd travelled 18 Miles over the worst road I ever saw and come to Boggy Depot and crossed 4 Rivers It is well Known by that name We hauled cattle out of the Mud with oxen half the day.

8th. traveled 4 miles and camped for the day to [wait] for 12 Beeves that is in another Heard. this is another gloomey evening and I tremble for the result of this night—Thunder and rain all night was in the saddle until day light am almost dead for sleep.

10th. Feel much refreshed this morning and am ready for the duties of the day crossed Elk and Canion Creeks and camped near S. Fork of Canadian.

12th. Hard Rain and Wind Big stampede and here we are among the Indians with 150 head of Cattle gone hunted all day and the Rain pouring down with but poor success Dark days are these to me Nothing but Bread and Coffee

Hands all Growling and Swearing—every thing wet and cold Beeves gone rode all day and gathered all but 35 Mixed with 8 other Herds Last night 5000 Beeves stampeded at this place and a general mix up was the result

14th. Last night there was a terrible storm Rain poured in torrents *all* night and up to 12 M today our Beeves left us in the night but for *once* on the whole trip we found them *all* together near camp at day break. *all* the other droves as far as I can hear are scattered to the four winds our Other Herd was all gone. We are now 25 Miles from Ark River and it is Very High we are water bound by two creeks and but Beef and Flour to eat. am not Homesick but Heart sick.

18th. Nice day went to Ft Gibson got some coffee and Beefe. River very High but falling. Gloomey prospect out of Money and provisions got back to camp and found the Indians had been there and claimed and tried to take some of our cattle. The Indians are making trouble stampeeding cattle here. We expect it. Cook dinner under a tree on the A K River Bank with two Ladies

19th. Good day 15 Indians come to Herd and tried to take some Beeves. Would not let them. Had a big muss One drew his Knife and I my revolver. Made them leave but fear they have gone for others they are the Seminoles.

23rd. worked all day hard in the River trying to make the Beeves swim and did not get one over. Had to go back to Prairie Sick and discouraged. Have *not* got the *Blues* but am in *Hel of a fix.* Indians held High Festival over stolen Beef all night. lost 2 Beeves mired and maby more.

25th. We hired 20 Indians to help us cross. We worked from Morning until 2 Oclock and finally got them over with a loss of 5 and camped near the *old* Mission between the Ark River and the Verdigris.

27th. Beautiful Bright Morn appearnce of warm day My Back is Blistered badly from exposure while in the River and I with two others are Suffering very much I was attacked by a Beefe in the River and had a very narrow escape from being hurt by Diving this day has been very warm travelled 10 Miles and rested.

July 9th. Still cloudy followed a man that drove off one of My Beeves and got him. Other Herd came up and went on. it camped 1½ Miles from us and that night at 9 Oclock it stampeded and ran one Mile and over. the next Morning.

18th. Spent the day trying to settle up with partners preparitory to starting around Kansas to get Home Horse stolen last night.

23rd. finished our settlement and divided our Beeves—drove 3 Miles and camped for the night. Made a contract with Mr. Bumbarger of Honey Grove Fanin Co Texas and Mr. Augustus Goff of Paris Lamar Co Texas who had 300 Stock cattle—to go through together and join Herds—

29th. Sunday Excitement in camp thought our Horses and oxen were stolen but found them after many troubles we got down the Mountain and across the Creek weather very *Hot* Travelled 8 miles Lost my coat and went back after it. Osages visited our camp Are great Beggars.

30th. Drove 6 Miles and crossed Verdigris had to give the Indians a Beefe for the right of way. Indians saucy Went Bathing 5 miles in afternoon and camp.

August 1st. No trouble last night but lost a Cow have travelled about 10 Miles today and while I sit here in the grass in the Broad prairie the Rear of the Herd is coming up Weather pleasant and no flies.

3rd. All right but 2 men one down with Boils and one with Ague Travelled about 10 Miles over high Rocky Peaks and 2 creeks with fine grass.

8th. Come to Big Walnut cattle stampeded and ran by 2 farms and the People were very angry but we made it all right was visited by Many Men was threatened with the Law but think we are all right now (Plenty of vegetables)

10. Separating cattle is the business of the day. Appearances of rain (no rain).

22d. We have travelled about 20 miles today and camped on Mill Creek I am on herd tonight it is now 11 oclock a beautiful moonlight night but cool. I have to stand half the night the day was *cold* and some rain—There is but little timber in all this country none only on the water courses there are some fine springs I have a severe pane in my neck

31st. Last night was one of those old fashioned rainy stormey thundering nights just such as we used to have in Texas was up with the cattle all night. They travelled where they pleased but we stuck too them until morning. Today we crossed Big Muddy and camped. . . . It commenced raining at dark and rained all night was up with cattle until midnight and then went to bed found them all in the morning.

October 3rd. Taylor and I left the Herd and started for Home.

from Giants in the Earth

O. E. Rölvaag

THE GREAT PLAIN DRINKS THE BLOOD OF CHRISTIAN MEN AND IS SATISFIED

I

Many and incredible are the tales the grandfathers tell from those days when the wilderness was yet untamed, and when they, unwittingly, founded the Kingdom. There was the Red Son of the Great Prairie, who hated the Palefaces with a hot hatred; stealthily he swooped down upon them, tore up and laid waste the little settlements. Great was the terror he spread; bloody the saga concerning him.

From **Giants in the Earth** by O. E. Rölvaag, pp. 110-116. Copyright © 1927 by Harper & Row, Publishers, Inc.; renewed 1955 by Jennie Marie Berdahl Rölvaag. Reprinted by permission of Harper & Row, Publishers, Inc.

But more to be dreaded than this tribulation was the strange spell of sadness which the unbroken solitude cast upon the minds of some. Many took their own lives; asylum after asylum was filled with disordered beings who had once been human. It is hard for the eye to wander from sky line to sky line, year in and year out, without finding a resting place! . . .

Then, too, there were the years of pestilence—toil and travail, famine and disease. God knows how human beings could endure it all. And many did not—they lay down and died. "There is nothing to do about that," said they who survived. "We are all destined to die—that's certain. Some must go now; others will have to go later. It's all the same, is it not?" The poor could find much wherewith to console themselves. And whisky was cheap in those days, and easy to get. . . .

And on the hot summer days terrible storms might come. In the twinkling of an eye they would smash to splinters the habitations which man had built for himself, so that they resembled nothing so much as a few stray hairs on a wornout pelt. Man have power? Breathe it not, for that is to tempt the Almighty! . . .

Some feared most the prairie fire. Terrible, too, it was, before people had learned how to guard against it.

Others remembered best the trips to town. They were the jolliest days, said some; no, they were the worst of all, said the others. It may be that both were right. . . . The oxen moved slowly—whether the distance was thirty miles or ninety made little difference. In the sod house back there, somewhere along the horizon, life got on your nerves at times. There sat a wife with a flock of starving children; she had grown very pale of late, and the mouths of the children were always open—always crying for food. . . . But in the town it was cheerful and pleasant. There one could get a drink; there one could talk with people who spoke with enthusiasm and certainty about the future. This was the land of promise, they said. Sometimes one met these people in the saloons; and then it was more fascinating to listen to them than to any talk about the millennium. Their words lay like embers in the mind during the whole of the interminable, jolting journey homeward, and made it less long. . . . It helps so much to have something pleasant to think about, say the Old.

And it was as if nothing affected people in those days. They threw themselves blindly into the Impossible, and accomplished the Unbelievable. If anyone succumbed in the struggle—and that happened often—another would come and take his place. Youth was in the race; the unknown, the untried, the unheard-of, was in the air; people caught it, were intoxicated by it, threw themselves away, and laughed at the cost. Of course it was possible—everything was possible out here. There was no such thing as the Impossible any more. The human race has not known such faith and such self-confidence since history began. . . . And so had been the Spirit since the day the first settlers landed on the eastern shores; it would rise and fall at intervals, would swell and surge on again with every new wave of settlers that rolled westward into the unbroken solitude.

II

They say it rained forty days and forty nights once in the old days, and that was terrible; but during the winter of 1880-81 it snowed twice forty days; that was more terrible.... Day and night the snow fell. From the 15th of October, when it began, until after the middle of April, it seldom ceased. From the four corners of the earth it flew; but of all the winds that brought it, the south wind was the worst; for that whisked and matted the flakes into huge grey discs, which fell to the ground in clinging, woolly folds.... And all winter the sun stayed in his house; he crept out only now and then to pack down the snow; that was to make room for more.... Morning after morning folk would wake up in the dead, heavy cold, and would lie in bed listening to the *ooo-h-ooo-h -ooo-h-ing* of the wind about the corners of the house. But what was this low, muffled roar in the chimney? One would leap out of bed, dress himself hurriedly in his heaviest garments, and start to go out—only to find that some one was holding the door. It wouldn't budge an inch. An immovable monster lay close outside. Against this monster one pushed and pushed, until one could scoop a little of the snow through the crack into the room; finally one was able to force an opening large enough for a man to work himself out and flounder up to the air. Once outside, he found himself standing in an immense flour bin, out of which whirled the whiteness, a solid cloud. Then he had to dig his way down to the house again. And tunnels had to be burrowed from house to barn, and from neighbour to neighbour, wherever the distances were not too long and where there were children who liked to play at such things.

In the late spring, when all this snow had to thaw, the floods would come, covering all the land. Once again it would be just as it had been in the days of Noah; on the roofs of houses, on the gables of barns, in wagon boxes, even, people would go sailing away. Many would perish—for there was no Ark in those days!...

The suffering was great that winter. Famine came; supplies of all kinds gave out; for no one had thought, when the first snowfall began, that winter had come. Who had ever heard of its setting in in the middle of the autumn?... And for a while not much snow did come; the fall was light in November, though the days were grey and chill; in December there was more; January began to pile and drift it up; and in February the very demon himself arrived. Some had to leave their potatoes in the ground; others could not thresh the grain; fuel, if not provided beforehand, was scarcely to be had at all; and it was impossible for anyone to get through to town to fetch what might be needed.

In the houses round about folks were grinding away at their own wheat; for little by little the flour had given out, and then they had to resort to the coffee mill. Everyone came to it—rich and poor alike. Those who had no mill of their own were forced to borrow; in some neighbourhoods there were as many as four families using one mill.

That winter Torkel Tallaksen had two newcomer boys working for their board; he also kept a hired girl; in addition to these he had a big family of his own, so that his supply of flour was soon exhausted. Now, he owned one mill, but he wasn't satisfied with that, so he went and borrowed four more; one might as well grind enough to last for a time while one was at it, he maintained. And so they ground away at his house for two days; but at the end of that time they were all so tired of it that they refused to grind any more.

When the mills had to be returned one of the little Tallaksen boys put on his skis and started off for Tönseten's with the one they had borrowed there. The slight thaw of the day before and the frost of the previous night had left a hard crust on the snow; in some places this would bear him up, but more often it was so thin that he broke through. Down by the creek the snowdrifts lay like mountains. Here the boy let himself go, gathered more speed than he had expected to, and went head over heels into a huge snowdrift. His skis flew one way, the mill another. When he tried to recover the mill he broke through the drift, and then both he and the mill were buried in snow. He dug himself out, began to hunt wildly for the mill, broke through again, floundered around, and at last managed to lose the mill completely. After hunting until he was tired, he had to give it up; there was nothing to do but to go to Tönseten and tell him what had happened.

"You haven't lost the mill?" gasped Tönseten, seriously alarmed.

"No," said the boy, laughing. He knew exactly where it was, but he just couldn't find it.

"And you laugh at that, you young idiot!" Tönseten was so angry that he boxed the boy's ears; then he pulled on his coat and rushed off to ask his neighbours to help him hunt for the lost treasure. It was on this occasion that he coined a saying that later became a by-word in the settlement—"Never mind your lives, boys, if you can only find the mill!"

But the greatest hardship of all for the settlers was the scarcity of fuel—no wood, no coal. In every home people sat twisting fagots of hay with which to feed the fire.

Whole herds of cattle were smothered in the snow. They disappeared during the great early storm in October, and were never seen again; when the snow was gone in the spring, they would reappear low on some hillside. After lying there for six months, they would be a horrible sight.

And the same thing happened to people: some disappeared like the cattle; others fell ill with the cough; people died needlessly, for want of a doctor's care; they did not even have the old household remedies—nothing of any kind. And when some one died, he was laid out in what the family could spare, and put away in a snowbank—until some later day. . . . There would be many burials in the settlement next spring.

The Lane County Bachelor

(Popular Song, 1890)

1

My name is Frank Bolar, 'nole bachelor I am,
I'm keepin' old bach on an elegant plan.
You'll find me out West in the County of Lane
Starving to death on a government claim;
My house it is built of the national soil,
The walls are erected according to Hoyle,
The roof has no pitch but is level and plain
And I always get wet when it happens to rain.

Chorus

But hurrah for Lane County, the land of the free,
The home of the grasshopper, bedbug, and flea,
I'll sing loud her praises and boast of her fame
While starving to death on my government claim.

2

My clothes they are ragged, my language is rough,
My head is case-hardened, both solid and tough;
The dough it is scattered all over the room
And the floor would get scared at the sight of a broom;
My dishes are dirty and some in the bed
Covered with sorghum and government bread;
But I have a good time, and live at my ease
On common sop-sorghum, old bacon and grease.

Chorus

But hurrah for Lane County, the land of the West,
Where the farmers and laborers are always at rest,
Where you've nothing to do but sweetly remain,
And starve like a man on your government claim.

3

How happy am I when I crawl into bed,
And a rattlesnake rattles his tail at my head,

And the gay little centipede, void of all fear,
Crawls over my pillow and into my ear,
And the nice little bedbug, so cheerful and bright,
Keeps me a scratching full half of the night,
And the gay little flea, with toes sharp as a tack,
Plays "Why don't you catch me?" all over my back.

Chorus

But hurrah for Lane County, where blizzards arise,
Where the winds never cease and the flea never dies,
Where the sun is so hot if in it you remain
'T will burn you quite black on your government claim.

4

How happy am I on my government claim,
Where I've nothing to lose and nothing to gain,
Nothing to eat and nothing to wear,
Nothing from nothing is honest and square.
But here I am stuck, and here I must stay,
My money's all gone and I can't get away;
There's nothing will make a man hard and profane
Like starving to death on a government claim.

Chorus

Then come to Lane County, there's room for you all,
Where the winds never cease and the rains never fall,
Come join in the chorus and boast of her fame,
While starving to death on your government claim.

5

Now don't get discouraged, ye poor hungry men,
We're all here as free as a pig in a pen;
Just stick to your homestead and battle your fleas,
And pray to your Maker to send you a breeze.
Now a word to claim-holders who are bound for to stay:
You may chew your hard-tack 'till you're toothless and gray,
But as for me, I'll no longer remain
And starve like a dog on my government claim.

Chorus

Farewell to Lane County, farewell to the West,
I'll travel back East to the girl I love best;
I'll stop in Missouri and get me a wife,
And live on corn dodgers the rest of my life.

The Gunfighter Legend

Joseph G. Rosa

It is noon. The sun blazes down on a sun-baked, dusty street. Except for an occasional cow pony standing with lowered head at a hitching rail, its tail switching idly at the ever-present flies, no living thing is to be seen. Suddenly the street is no longer deserted. Two men have walked out from the shade of buildings some fifty yards apart. Almost casually they step to the center of the street and stand facing each other. They begin to move forward slowly but steadily, spurs jingling softly, boot heels raising small clouds of dust.

One of the men carries himself arrogantly erect, his lips drawn back in a sneer, aware that hidden along the street are people watching him with hate—a hatred born of fear. His expression is contemptuous as his hand hovers near the butt of an ornate six-shooter that flashes brightly in the harsh rays of the sun with each movement of his body. His eyes are snakelike, unblinking, cold, and cruel. For he is a killer, determined that the man now approaching him shall die—as all others have died who have dared to challenge him or his ruthless ambition. But he is also fearful because he knows that the man he is facing represents everything that he is not.

The other man is tall, and his well-proportioned body moves with a panther-like grace as he paces down the street. Looking neither to the right nor to the left, he walks with deadly purpose toward his antagonist. His features are grim, his mouth a taut slash marring a normally handsome face. His blue-gray eyes, usually relaxed and smiling, are now implacable as they watch the man ahead. At each step his hands brush against the polished butts of twin Colt .45's nested in holsters hanging low from crossed cartridge belts. The lower ends of the holsters are lashed to his thighs with rawhide thongs to give him just that extra speed on the draw which might mean the difference between life and death. Staring mortality in the face, he dare not show fear as he stalks toward the man whose depravity has led to this duel to the death. On him depend the future of the town and the welfare of the people who at this moment are crouching in the shadows, fearfully awaiting the next seconds.

From **The Gunfighter: Man or Myth?** by Joseph G. Rosa. Copyright 1969 by the University of Oklahoma Press.

Hands flash down, and the thunderous roar of heavy Colts fills the air. When the acrid blue smoke clears, our hero stands alone, guns in hand, his enemy dead in the dust. Once more good has triumphed over evil. From the shadows of the buildings people slowly emerge to shake his hand and thank him for saving them. This is the hero of countless Western movies and novels—the big, sometimes cruel, magnificent demigod we call the "gunfighter."

There is no Western legend as enduring as that of the overrated gunfighter. He is the embodiment of every hero of all time, and yet no one can say for sure what really inspired his legend. It is not enough to say that he was a product of the time. What is there about this figure that has such mass appeal? Principally it is his character that attracts such a wide audience. Modern society's organizations devoted to law and order attempt to apprehend and punish the wrongdoer when crimes against persons or property are committed, but this is normally a long-drawn-out process, and the results are not always satisfactory. In real life individuals are not allowed to take the law into their own hands, but in fiction the legendary gunfighter can act as judge, jury, and executioner. In him people see themselves reacting to similar situations.

In a Western movie or book all manner of injustices are put right by the gunfighter hero, a two-gun Galahad whose pistols are always at the service of those in trouble. Tales of his heroic exploits and of feats impossible for man and weapon have stimulated a world-wide interest in the Amercan West. Since it is essential that the gunfighter's pistol prowess be beyond reproach, he is gifted with phenomenal reflexes which enable him to draw and fire a revolver with incredible speed and accuracy. There is no room for any weakness in his legend.

The instrument of a gunfighter's appeal is his pistol. Without it he is meaningless, for the gun signifies his strength and purpose. In his hands it is the tool of justice or destruction, each shot finding its mark, for "Judge Colt and his jury of six" is unerring in its verdict of death to wrongdoers. No other make of revolver has enjoyed the fame of the Colt, both as a military arm and as a Western civilizer. Of the many different guns used in the West, the gunfighter's particular favorite was the 1873 Army model, the Peacemaker—without doubt the most famous firearm ever made. A six-shot single-action (that is, cocked by hand for each shot) revolver, it became the instrument of both lawmaker and lawbreaker during the last twenty-five years of the nineteenth century and is today an integral part of the gunfighter legend. Weighing just over three pounds fully loaded, well balanced and hard-hitting, it was an ideal fighting man's weapon.

Belief in the superhuman skill of gunfighters and their weapons is not restricted to modern times. In the heyday of the Old West particular attention was paid to a man's ability with a six-shooter. In 1879 a Cheyenne newspaper described the accomplishments of "Wild Bill" Hickok with his cap-and-ball Colt revolvers. The "Prince of Pistoleers" had been dead but three years; nevertheless, his legendary marksmanship was firmly fixed in the public mind:

His ivory handled revolvers . . . were made expressly for him and were finished in a manner unequalled by any ever before manufactured in this or any other country. It is said that a bullet from them never missed its mark. Remarkable stories are told of the dead shootist's skill with these guns. He could keep two fruit cans rolling, one in front and one behind him, with bullets fired from these firearms. This is only a sample story of the hundreds which are related of his incredible dexterity with these revolvers.[1]

The Western town of books and movies usually has only one street, flanked by dust-covered, sun-drenched, false-fronted buildings—the marshal's office, a saloon, a bank, and sometimes a general store. Almost always the saloon, where good in the form of the gunfighter has its first meeting with evil, is the center of the stage. Here the villain—a rustler, outlaw, or other undesirable whose hold on the town threatens its existence—holds court. Nobody seems to be employed except the bartender, who is forever polishing glasses or pushing bottles to the loafers who are awaiting the inevitable tragedy that will take place during the last five minutes of the story.

On the rare occasions when there is any insight into the characters of the protagonists, it is quickly apparent that they are both something more and something less than human. This situation in the movie Western creates stereotyped characters that eventually begin to pall on the most ardent of fans. In many television and movie Westerns the hero appears to have little or no interest in the opposite sex. Most of the time he leans against a post outside the marshal's office or perches on the hitching rail alongside the saloon, watching all that goes on. The villain plots the acquisition of a ranch, a bank robbery, or some other nefarious scheme which will force the men into open conflict. . . .

A desire to preserve the gunfighter legend, a refusal to let the old days die, served to give the legend another twist—the fast draw. All over the United States and in many parts of the world this feat has captured the imagination of gun lovers and Old West fans. In a little less than a hundred years the gunfighter legend has turned full circle. *Beadle's Dime Novels,* Buffalo Bill's wild West shows, and modern Western novels, movies, and television shows all contributed to the myth. Admirers of the fast draw, caring not that the supposed originator wore a tarnished halo, elevate his modern counterpart to a kind of sainthood. Feats of speed and marksmanship attributed to the legendary gunfighter are duplicated and bettered by modern-day marksmen. For many people the fast draw is an inseparable part of the cult of the six-shooter.

In place of the early-day leather holsters, built for the dual purpose of carrying and protecting a pistol, modern fast-draw holsters are steel-lined, cut away to a minimum, and specially molded to fit the gun. Some are even designed to allow the cylinder to turn so that the gun can be cocked in the holster by the heel of the hand. The time taken to draw and fire one shot has improved considerably since Ed McGivern set his record of .25 seconds in 1934—and thereby helped create general interest in the fast draw.

---

1. Cheyenne Daily Leader, July 1, 1879.

The fast draw, which really caught on in 1954, seems to have been the creation of Dee Woolem, who practiced fast draw between acts at his job of "robbing" an excursion train at a tourist exhibition in Orange County, California. He built an electric timer to time his speed, and others copied him. Within five years the fast draw had aroused nation-wide interest. By the middle 1960s the fast draw had practitioners around the world. Today competitions are held to determine the "fastest gun alive" among the synthetic gunfighters, and the competition is very keen. There are rules and strict supervision to ensure that no one uses anything but blanks or wax bullets. Whether one condones or condemns the fast draw, it does illustrate the fantastic appeal of the legendary gunfighter and his weapons.

The old-time gunfighters and the modern-day fast-draw addicts have one thing in common—similar weapons. There the similarity ends. The gunfight was a fact; the fast draw, a fantasy.

The fast draw has become the subject of controversy among target shooters and others devoted to various forms of sport shooting. Many dedicated sportsmen regard it as childish and irresponsible and damaging to the sport of shooting. This view is reinforced by the antics of the lunatic fringe, who really believe that their speed identifies them with the early-day westerners. Disparagers of the cult take the more realistic view expressed by a much-respected authority in the gun world, who summed it up as follows:

I have never happened to meet a Fast Draw addict who claimed he could excel the old timers in guts, but when a good one tells you that he can excel the old timers in speed, he's 100 percent right! I know a hundred men who can draw, fire, and hit a target in less time than Hickok or any old timer could ever have done. I know this can't be proved, simply because no old timer ever was timed. But it must certainly be accepted—because no old timer ever had the gun or the holster essential to such speeds. Hickok, with his sash-held guns, would have been blown apart before he could get those guns clear, given a face to face test against today's speedsters. I don't say the modern boys would have killed him—that's a very different kettle of fish. Almost everyone, in a kill situation, is reluctant to shoot. I would expect most of today's fast gunmen to draw, see that they had the opponent hopelessly beaten, and stop, expecting him to accept defeat. Whereupon Hickok (or Hardin, or Earp, or Breakenridge, et al.) would proceed to kill him! Because I don't believe those men *had* much, if any, such reluctance!

But I know several modern gunmen who could and would kill any one of the old timers, given their own modern equipment against that of the old timers. Only a few days ago, I saw Bill Jordan (Captain, Border Patrol, and a noted exhibition shooter and fast draw artist), hold a coin on the back of his right hand at less than shoulder height, drop his hand from under the coin, draw (with the same hand), and intercept the coin with the barrel of the gun at hip level. The coin dropped not more than 14 inches;

you can figure the speed of the draw. This was done in a motel room; but I have seen Jordan do this with a loaded gun, let the coin drop past his gun and then hit it with a bullet before it touched the floor. No old time gunman ever approached this speed; and I say Jordan not only could but would have killed them, because Jordan has killed a few men himself, in the course of some 35 years of law enforcement.

Actually, there never were any face to face, Hollywood-type, draw-and-shoot duels between known old timers. And if there had been, between men of anything like equal skill, the man who *started* to draw first would always win. Why? Simply because it takes even a man with quick reactions 20 to 25 hundredths of a second to respond to any "signal." And hundreds of today's gunmen can draw, fire, and hit in half a second or less. . . . If Gunman A waited for Gunman B to "go for his gun," Gunman B's starting movement would be Gunman A's starting signal. It will take him 20 hundredths of a second, at the very least, to see that signal and react to it by starting for his own gun. If both men can draw, fire, and hit in half a second, Gunman B will beat Gunman A by 20 hundredths of a second, right? . . . You *can* set up a fair draw-and-shoot duel, only by letting both men get set, then giving both a starting signal. This way, and this way only, can they match their reaction time-gun dexterity speed. And I never heard of this being done, in the Old West. Nobody then was splitting seconds into fractions; and nobody then ever thought of such a thing as "reaction time." (A good fast draw man will have you stand facing him with your open hands a foot apart, tell you to clap your hands when you see him start to move—and then draw and put his gun between your hands before you can clap them—merely proving that his draw speed excels your reaction time.) . . .

I agree with you that the methods of handgun combat of today and those of Hickok's era are a world apart. We know the old timers tried for some degree of speed in getting their guns into action, even dreaming up trick ways of carrying the guns to permit quicker shots—such things as bottomless holsters, guns worn with no holsters at all but with metal studs fitting into metal sockets on the belt to permit swiveling the gun to firing position, etc. Hickok's own carry must have been aimed toward quickness, among other things. But nobody ever, in those days, came up with any holster or any method of carrying that approached the speed potential of modern, steel-stiffened holsters; and, as you say (and in spite of all the fictional poppycock about giving the other guy the first move), the old timers took a pretty practical approach to the problems of getting a gun into action. . . .

The Captain Jordan mentioned above has written a book on the subject of guns and shooting from a policeman's point of view and has explained at length the difficulties in deciding when and when not to draw a gun, in action or in preparation for action. Perhaps his most pertinent remark was, "Speed's fine but accuracy's final."

from The Negro Cowboys

Philip C. Durham and Everett L. Jones

[Until quite recently virtually all Western novels and films portrayed an exclusively White, Anglo-Saxon frontier. The only significant non-Whites were ferocious Indians. Occasionally a stereotyped Mexican peon or a Chinese coolie was added for "comic relief," but the heroic parts—the conquerors of the plains—were always left for Whites. The writings that poured out of the real West from 1870-1890 (everything from news articles to letters to the paintings of Charles Russel and Frederic Remington), indicate that the lily-white frontier never really existed at all. The Chinese were the key labor force in building America's transcontinental railroads. Mexican-Americans have been a vital factor in the economic and political development of the Southwest throughout the nineteenth and twentieth centuries. Most neglected of all, however, have been the Black participants in the Westward movement. Thousands of Afro-Americans pioneered the territory west of the Mississippi, serving as cattle drovers, farmers, cavalry soldiers (the U.S. 10th and 11th regiments who policed the plains were exclusively Black), and lawmen. Yet our cowboy folklore renders them invisible.

The significant role of the Black frontiersman in the development of the American West has been analyzed by Philip Durham and Everett Jones in their detailed book, *The Negro Cowboys.* Here, in an excerpt from that book, is an example of the role of the Black man in the real West.]

George W. Saunders, at one time president of the Old Time Trail Drivers Association, estimated that from 1868 to 1895 "fully 35,000 men went up the trail with herds," and of this number "about one-third were negroes and Mexicans."

When nationality or color is mentioned in accounts of the trail drives, far more Negroes than Mexicans are identified. It also appears that Mexicans, although many of them were excellent vaqueros, adapted themselves less well than Negroes to the long drives. They suffered from prejudices nearly as strong as those that worked against Negroes, and they had a language handicap. Unlike the Negroes, who could expect some protection from the law during Reconstruction days, as well as active sympathy from some old Abolitionists in Kansas,

Nebraska and other northern states, the Mexicans were despised foreigners in a strange land. Unlike the Negroes, who found that provisions for Negro troops had opened restaurants, saloons and even whorehouses to them, the Mexicans could expect to find themselves welcome only at the gambling tables. Small wonder, then, that Mexicans appear infrequently in accounts of the drives to Abilene, Dodge City and Cheyenne.

Yet even if all these evidences are discounted, and even if large numbers of Mexican vaqueros are assumed to have ridden the Chisholm Trail, the Western Trail and other trails north, it seems safe to assume that more than five thousand Negro cowboys rode north out of Texas during the three decades following the Civil War.

Understandably, most of the men who wrote of their days on the plains did not designate color or nationality among the cowboys with whom they rode. One finds reminiscences in which a cowboy is introduced by name as one of many others and then several pages later is identified, almost by chance, as a Negro. But from a sampling of writers who seemingly did note race or nationality with some consistency, one can infer that a typical trail crew had among its eight cowboys two or three Negroes. Its boss was almost certain to be white, although a few Negroes led crews up the trail. Its wrangler might be Negro or Mexican. Its cook was likely to be a Negro—usually an ex-cowboy.

A careful reader of Western reminiscences can note frequent references to Negro cowboys. Many of these, retold or quoted in various parts of this book, deal with stampedes, gunfights, snakebites, stomachaches, Indian attacks, jailbreaks and other adventures or misadventures. But some are simple listings. William G. Butler drove to Abilene in 1868 with a crew of twelve men that included Mexicans, white Texans and two Negroes, Levi and William Perryman. On a similar trip, Joseph S. Cruze had Adam Rector, a Negro "who could ride and rope with the best," as his "main helper." At least one Negro was in the crew that helped Richard Withers drive thirty-five hundred head to Abilene in 1870. George Hindes rode in 1872 with eight Mexicans and one Negro, Jack Hopkins. On drives to Kansas in 1873, C. W. Ackerman rode with seven white men and one Negro, while R. F. Galbreath traveled with four white men and three Negroes. In 1874, the same year that George Chapman rode through a stampede with old Chief, a Negro, L. B. Anderson was also in a crew with a Negro cowhand. In early March of the same year, Jim Ellison went up the trail with all Negro hands.

Other listings are typical. In the middle seventies near the Kansas line Charlie Siringo rode point with "Negro Gabe." G. W. Mills trailed to Ogallala in 1877 with "the following boys, not a one over twenty-three years of age: W. M. Ellison, son of the boss; E. F. Hilliard, W. F. Felder, E. M. Storey, Albert McQueen, Ace Jackson, . . . two negro cowhands and a negro cook." A story of a drive a year later mentions a Negro cowboy, Thad, only because he happened to find a large box of snuff in an area where "at least nine women out of ten" used it. He sold it for a good price at Red River Station. Eight riders, "two of them colored," were engaged by George Gilland to take his herd from Texas to

Wyoming in 1882. And in 1885 Lytle & Stevens sent a herd up the trail "bossed by Al Jones, a negro."

The catalog could continue for pages. Only now and then does a bare list or reference hint at an untold story. What, for instance, is hidden in the laconic note written by Henry D. Steele in 1920? He wrote: "It has been just thirty-seven years since I went over the trail. I do not know what has become of the men who went with me on that trip. One of the hands, Charlie Hedgepeth, the negro, was hanged at Sequin by a mob some years ago." Another Negro cowboy, George Glenn, is the only man identified in the crew that R. B. Johnson took from Colorado County, Texas, to Abilene in 1870. Shortly after reaching Abilene, Johnson died, his body was embalmed, and he was buried in Kansas. The following September the body was disinterred, and George Glenn took his old boss home. Because there were no railroads leading from Kansas to Texas, Glenn loaded the body in a Studebaker wagon and drove it back, making a trip that took forty-two days, sleeping every night in the wagon by the casket.

The Problem of Indian Leadership

Vine Deloria, Jr.

[Few have suffered more from the folklore of the Western novel and movies than the American Indian. Most of the time we see him as a painted, animalistic barbarian. He is the scourge of the frontier, the eternal sub-human enemy. Occasionally, however, he turns up as a good guy—a noble, loyal savage, who aids the White hero (or better yet, heroine) against his villainous brethren. But whether the Indian is the evil Geronimo of countless Western movies, or the lovable Tonto ("Friendly Indian Companion of the Masked Man . . ."), he has always been a stereotype.

Vine Deloria, Jr., a Sioux Indian, has brilliantly destroyed the simple-minded stereotypes of American Indians in his best-selling book, *Custer Died for Your Sins: An Indian Manifesto.* In the segment of his book which follows, Deloria discusses the White mythology surrounding the Indians of the plains and how it developed.]

Quite early in the Civil Rights struggle certain individuals emerged and were accepted as representative leaders of the Negro people. Martin Luther King, James Farmer, Bayard Rustin, Whitney Young, John Lewis, and others were able to attract the attention of the communications media. It was largely through identification with these individuals that vast numbers of Americans began to be concerned about Civil Rights. By vicariously experiencing the exploits of King and others, people participated in the great marches and felt they had an important emotional investment in the outcome. For a time, at least, racial themes were submerged by the common appeal for simple justice.

When the Civil Rights goals became blurred and a multitude of leaders appeared to be saying contradictory things, public sympathy vanished as quickly as it had arisen. No longer could people identify with simply understood individuals who stood for simple goals.

Indians experienced an era similar to the Civil Rights movement in the closing years of the last century. Then Indian tribes and their great leaders dominated the news and attracted the attention of the public. The Indian struggle for freedom was symbolized by the great war chiefs Crazy Horse, Sitting Bull, Chief Joseph, and Geronimo. They were better known than the important statesmen of those days. Public interest often reached a fever pitch and opinions were as evenly divided as to solutions to the Indian problem then as they are today about the Negro problem.

Public opinion was fickle. When Custer was wiped out the impulse was to exterminate the Sioux. Yet several years later Sitting Bull was so popular that he appeared in Wild West shows. Chief Joseph, the great Nez Perce chief, left his reservation in Oregon with his people and headed for the Canadian border. Whites were terrified at first. Later they cheered for the Nez Perces as they eluded troop after troop of cavalry. When they were finally caught twelve miles from the Canadian border nearly everyone in the nation was on their side. Even the opposing generals, who had the task of catching the tribe, were attracted by Joseph's obvious ability to command.

The Cheyennes were corraled on a dusty reservation in Oklahoma and longed for their homeland in Montana. Facing starvation on their desert lands in the South, the tribe broke for freedom. They managed to elude the major cavalry forces that were sent out to catch them and got through Kansas unnoticed. In Nebraska the troops finally caught up and killed most of them. A few kept going and reached Montana. Some hid with Red Cloud's Oglala Sioux at Pine Ridge, South Dakota, where they were given refuge. When the public realized the tragedy of Dull Knife and his starving band of homeward-fleeing Cheyennes, the tide turned in favor of the tribes. They were able to survive by submitting to confined reservations and the ration system, and were eventually freed from the fear of physical extermination.

For a time the government attempted to break the power of the great war chiefs and failing, adopted the tactic of exile and assassination to render the Indian people completely docile. Once they were restricted to the reservations the might of the government was applied to the Indians to destroy their political and social institutions. Missionaries and government agents worked to undermine the influence of the old people and the medicine men. Of all the great Indian leaders perhaps only Red Cloud of the Oglala Sioux maintained his influence in his tribe until his death.

After the war chiefs had been killed or rendered harmless, Indians seemed to drift into a timeless mist. There appeared to be no leaders with which the general public could identify. The status of the Indian became a nebulous question which seemed familiar and important but for which there was apparently no answer.

Missionaries soon filled the vacuum through clever exploitation of natives who had turned Christian. There began in the East the great round of testimonial appearances of native clergymen who made speeches appealing for more missionary work among their tribes. Church congregations, indoctrinated with the message of the White Man's Burden, cooed with satisfaction to hear formerly fierce and feathered warriors relate how they had found the Lord and been brought out of their pagan darkness.

Poor things, so great had been the pressure on them to conform to the white man's way that they could do nothing else if they and their people were to survive. Only the fickle sentimentality of the churches often stood between them and the government policy of total dispersal or extinction of their people.

But the Christianized warrior role did not provide any significant means by which white people could identify with the real desires and needs of the Indian people. The post-pagans simply recited what they had been taught concerning their people's needs. Indian beliefs held most tenaciously were forbidden subjects and there was no way to attract the sympathy of the public to support ideas that were considered foreign.

After the turn of the century, Jim Thorpe almost overnight changed the image of the Indian in the mind of the public. Suddenly the Indian as the superathlete dominated the scene. This concept was soon replaced by the Indian as a show business personality with the rise to popularity of Will Rogers, the Cherokee humorist.

In large measure the Indian path to visibility has been paralleled by the Negro. A mythology created to explain Jim Thorpe and Will Rogers was later applied to Joe Louis and Dick Gregory in order to make Negroes comprehensible when they began to appear in American life. After the Indian had been accepted as a humorous, athletic, subspecies of white man, historians and popular writers revisited the past and carved out a role for the Indian that overlooked the centuries of bloodshed between white and red, effectively neutralizing historical betrayals of the Indian by the government.

The supreme archetype of the white Indian was born one day in the pulp magazines. This figure would not only dominate the pattern of what Indians had been and would be, but also actually block efforts to bring into focus the crises being suffered by Indian tribes.

It was Tonto—the Friendly Indian Companion—who galloped onto the scene, pushing the historical and the contemporary Indians into obscurity.

Tonto was everything that the white man had always wanted the Indian to be. He was a little slower, a little dumber, had much less vocabulary, and rode a darker horse. Somehow Tonto was always *there.* Like the Negro butler and the Oriental gardener, Tonto represented a silent subservient subspecies of Anglo-Saxon whose duty was to do the bidding of the all-wise white hero.

The standard joke, developed as group consciousness arose, had the Lone

Ranger and Tonto surrounded by a tribe of hostile Indians, with Tonto inquiring of the Lone Ranger, "Well, White Man?" The humor came from Tonto's complete departure from his stereotype. The real Tonto would have cut down his relatives with a Gatling gun rather than have a hair on said Ranger's head mussed.

But Tonto never rebelled, never questioned the Lone Ranger's judgment, never longed to go back to the tribe for the annual Sun Dance. Tonto was a cultureless Indian for Indians and an uncultured Indian for whites.

Tonto cemented in the minds of the American public the cherished falsehood that all Indians were basically the same—friendly and stupid. Indeed, the legend grew, not only were tribes the same, but all Indians could be brought to a state of grace—a reasonable facsimile of the white—by a little understanding.

But Tonto also had another quality about him. Although inarticulate to a fault, he occasionally called upon his primitive wisdom to get the Lone Ranger out of a tight spot. Tonto had some indefinable aboriginal knowledge that operated deus ex machina in certain situations. It was almost as if the Lone Ranger had some tragic flaw with respect to the mysterious in nature which Tonto could easily handle and understand.

In those crises where Tonto had to extricate the Lone Ranger by some impossibly Indian trick, a glimmer of hope was planted in the subconscious of the Indian that someday he would come into his own. Few whites realized what this was, or that it existed; but to Indians it was an affirmation of the old Indian way. In an undefined sense, Tonto was able to universalize Indianness for Indians and lay the groundwork for the eventual rejection of the white man and his strange ways.

And so when no one succeeded Thorpe and Rogers, Tonto cornered the market as the credible Indian personality. Turncoats of history who could be resurrected as examples of the "friendly Indian companion" were publicized in an attempt to elaborate on the Tonto image.

Squanto, who had welcomed the Pilgrims and helped them destroy the tribes in Connecticut and Long Island, was reworked as a "friendly" Indian as opposed to Massasoit, the father of King Philip the Wampanoag chief, who had suspicions about the Pilgrims from the very start.

Keokuk, the Sac and Fox subchief who had betrayed Black Hawk during the war which bears his name, was also brought back to life as a friendly companion. Washakie, the Shoshone chief who tattled on the other tribes every chance he got and finally received a nice reservation in Wyoming, was another early fink who was honored posthumously as a good guy.

Eastern society matrons somehow began to acquire blood from John Smith and Pocahontas. The real Indian leaders who had resisted the encroachments of the white man and died protecting their homes, became sullen renegades unworthy of note.

Both whites and Indians were buried under the weight of popular pseudo-history in which good guys dominated the scene and tribes were indiscriminately scattered throughout the West in an effort to liven up the story. Contemporary

Indian leadership was suppressed by tales of the folk heroes of the past. Attempts to communicate contemporary problems were brushed aside in favor of the convenient and comfortable pigeonhole into which Indians had been placed. The Sioux warbonnet, pride of the Plains Indians, became the universal symbol of Indianism. Even tribes that had never seen an eagle were required to wear a warbonnet to prove their lineage as Indians.

It was probably only because Indians were conveniently forgotten that a movement for national unity of all tribes became a possibility. So rigid was the stereotype of the friendly childlike Indian that all efforts by Indians to come together were passed off as the prattling of children who could not possibly do anything without instructions from their white friends.

Indian tribes were thus freed to experiment with the concept of inter-tribal unity because they were considered irrelevant. First on regional levels, occasionally with regional congresses, then finally on a national basis, tribes began to come together. They soon learned to use the prejudices of the friendly whites to their own advantage.

Reconstruction of past traitors as good Indians also brought with it remembrances of previous attempts to unify the tribes and repel the white invaders. Indian unity had been an old dream. Deganawidah had forged the great Iroquois confederacy out of a miscellaneous group of refugee tribes who had been driven out of the Missouri-Arkansas area in the fifteenth century by the stronger Osage and Quapaw tribes. Eventually this conglomeration dominated the northern portion of the United States completely. They were the balance of power in the colonial wars between England and France.

In the South the Creek confederacy had controlled a vast area in what is now Georgia, Mississippi, and Alabama with extensions of its power well into northern Florida. The Natchez confederacy ruled the Mississippi River plains almost completely and extended its influence a considerable distance southwestward.

With the westward movement of whites, temporary alliances were formed for the purpose of protecting hunting grounds. Pontiac and later Tecumseh brought the tribes together for momentary successes against the whites. But always it was too late with too little. Nowhere was there enough time for effective groupings to be built which guaranteed more than sporadic success.

In the Great Plains, traditional hunting alliances did their best to prevent white encroachment on their hunting grounds, but they could not stem the tide. The Sioux, Cheyenne, and Arapaho united briefly to send Custer on his way. But shortly after the battle the tribes split into a number of small bands which were all rounded up and placed on reservations by the following winter.

In the southern plains the Kiowa and Comanche had occasional successes before being overcome and sent to their western Oklahoma reservation. The desert areas saw the Paiutes and Shoshones futilely oppose the white man but quickly give in. The Northwest had a brief Yakima war and an even briefer struggle by Chief Joseph and his Nez Perces.

By and large the hunting economy was so entrenched that the destruction of the buffalo eliminated the economic base by which tribal alliances were cemented. The tribes seemed doomed to follow the buffalo. No large number of people could be kept together because they could not be fed. Thus sustained warfare was impossible for the tribes while still a way of life for the white man. In separate groups the tribes were easily defeated and confined to reservations through a series of so-called peace treaties. In fact, treaties were ultimatums dictated by historical reality. While the tribes could have fought on, absolute extinction would have been their fate.

Because buffalo and other game were so essential to the tribes, hunting areas defined the manner in which tribes would fight and where. It was fairly easy to divide and conquer the various tribes by exploiting their rivalry over hunting grounds. This the white man did with deadly and consummate skill. Indian warfare was oriented toward protection of food supply and courageous exploits. Sustained warfare to protect or control territory which they could not settle was inconceivable to most of the tribes. Killing others simply to rid the land of them was even more unthinkable. Thus the white man's way of war was the deadly antithesis of the Indian's.

From Plymouth Rock to the lava beds of northern California, the white man divided and conquered as easily as if he were slicing bread. The technique was not used simply to keep different tribes from uniting, but also to keep factions of the same tribe quarreling so that when their time came they would be unable to defend themselves. And most important, the United States government used the treaty as an ultimate weapon to destroy the tribal political institutions by recognizing some men as chiefs and refusing to recognize others.

In treating for lands, rights of way, and minerals, commissioners negotiating for the government insisted on applying foreign political concepts to the tribes they were confronting. Used to dealing with kings, queens, and royalty, the early white men insisted on meeting the supreme political head of each tribe. When they found none, they created one and called the man they had chosen *the Chief.*

Finding a chief at treaty-signing time was no problem. The most pliable man who could be easily bribed was named chief and the treaty was signed. Land cessions were often made and a tribe found itself on the way to a treeless desert before it knew what had happened. Most of the Indian wars began because of this method of negotiation. The Indians were always at a loss to explain what had happened. They got mad when told to move off lands which they had never sold and so they fought. Thus were renegades created.

Most tribes had never defined power in authoritarian terms. A man consistently successful at war or hunting was likely to attract a following in direct proportion to his continuing successes. Eventually the men with the greatest followings composed an informal council which made important decisions for the group. Anyone was free to follow or not, depending upon his own best judgment. The people only followed a course of action if they were convinced it was best for them. This was as close as most tribes ever got to a formal government.

In an absolutely democratic social structure like the Indian tribe, formal legal negotiations and contractual arrangements were nearly out of the question. Once a man's word was given it bound him because of his integrity, not because of what he had written on a sheet of paper.

Men went to war because they had faith in a leader, not because they were drafted to do so or because they had signed a paper pledging themselves to be hired killers for a set period of time. Indians had little respect for white generals who did not lead their men into battle and contemptuously tagged the first white soldiers they saw as the "men who take orders from the chief who is afraid to fight."

The basic Indian political pattern has endured despite efforts by the federal government to change it. The people still follow a man simply because he produces. The only difference between two centuries ago and today is that now the Bureau of Indian Affairs defines certain ground rules by which leaders can be changed. These rules are called tribal elections. Otherwise, leadership patterns have not changed at all.

Today a man holds his chairmanship as long as he produces, or at least appears to produce, for his tribe. Without making substantial progress or having the ability to present a fighting image, a man's term in tribal office is short and severe. Demands are great. Some tribes have never had an incumbent re-elected because tribal goals far surpass any conceivable performance. A few tribes have had strong men dominate tribal affairs for long periods of time because of their tremendous following with the people. . . .

FOR DISCUSSION

1. Compare the factual material in this section to any standard Western movie you may have seen. How do the actual descriptions of the Western plains differ from your concept of a "typical" Western setting? Why wouldn't the farmers, immigrants, and cattle drovers described here make good traditional Western heroes?

2. Before reading the rest of the material in this volume, speculate about how some of the myths about our Western heritage developed. Why have we created a fast-draw gunfighter who never really existed at all? Why have our images of the West excluded Blacks, and stereotyped other minorities? (Later in your reading, compare your responses here to the material in forthcoming sections of this book.)

3. After reading Vine Deloria's piece on "Indian Leadership" explain why we so thoroughly misunderstood Indian political structure. Consider particularly the Indian concepts of warfare and tribal political power. Try to create a short story or film script depicting Indian authority as Deloria describes it, avoiding the noble savage, "Uncle Tomahawk" stereotypes of chieftains.

PART TWO

The West As Fiction—
The Literary Myth

THE DIME NOVEL AND THE ESTABLISHMENT COWBOY

Long before the days of the cowboys of the silver screen, America had heroic images of Westerners. In the late nineteenth and early twentieth centuries, as the literacy rate in the country increased, the "dime novel" became America's first best-selling book format. Dime novels were a combination of today's sensationalistic paperbacks (without the sex) and the traditional comic book. Loaded with illustrations, written on an elementary level, and relatively inexpensive, these novels provided millions of people with a romantic escape from the tedium of everyday life in an increasingly industrialized society.

The most popular of the dime novels were the Westerns, detailing the exploits of the likes of Buffalo Bill, Jesse James, and "General" Custer.

During the twentieth century, the dime novel became a little more sophisticated (and expensive) and took the form of most hard-cover books. Its style and characters remained the same, however, and popular magazines often serialized these books, reaching an even wider audience.

Reprinted in this section is a detailed history of the dime novel Western, a thorough illustration of the pre-movie origins of the Western myth, by historian Henry Nash Smith.

The popularity of the Western myth can be traced even beyond the dime novelists to more sophisticated roots. Three Eastern gentlemen of wealth, education, and breeding helped legitimize the cowboy's image and make him into America's "knight in shining armor." Theodore Roosevelt, Frederic Remington, and Owen Wister had many things in common. Fellow Easterners (Roosevelt and Remington from New York state, Wister from Philadelphia) and peers in age, wealth, and status (they were also quite close friends), the three men lived in the far West for only short periods of their early adulthood. Still, each came away fascinated with the freedom of Western life. Each interpreted this as a kind of natural alternative to the unexciting, industrialized society of the East. Members of a disillusioned upper-class establishment, they saw the great plains as a sanctuary from their "enemies," the urban middle class and waves of foreign immigrants.

Theodore Roosevelt is, of course, best known for his political career. But in his early twenties he wrote a voluminous "history" of the Westward movement (*The Winning of the West*), which glorified the courage of the land-grabbing pioneer, the cowboy, and the Indian killer. He reached these conclusions after less than three years of ranching in the Dakotas before returning to the East for good.

Frederic Remington is best remembered as an artist for his life-like sketches and paintings of Western life. His work is a vivid and exciting portrait of the Old West, even though Remington himself only spent about two years on a Kansas ranch. Much of his work is based on detailed research, rather than first-hand observation.

Owen Wister spent only a few years in Wyoming in the 1880s yet he immortalized the cowboy as a Sir Galahad of the plains with his best-selling novel, *The Virginian* (1902). This book, the subject of a play, two films, and a popular television show, created an image of the cowboy which is now standardized. Historian Samuel Eliot Morison describes Wister's contribution to Western lore in this way:

> Wister created the literary cliché of the gentle cowpuncher who respected virtuous womanhood . . . defending the free open life of the range against homesteaders and other bad men who were trying to destroy it. He was the progenitor of standardized Western literature, of the rodeos for which horses are trained to buck, and the so-called "horse opera" on radio and in the movies, which have made the fortunes of hack and script writers. This distorted image of the American Far West has traveled around the world; small boys in Europe, Asia, and Africa are still listening to these impossible tales of the Wild West and sporting imitations of Levi overalls, spurs, colt revolvers, and "ten-gallon hats."[1]

The motives of these three members of the Eastern upper class for glorifying the West are examined in the second part of this section by historian G. Edward White.

---

1. Samuel Eliot Morison, **The Oxford History of the American People** (New York: Oxford University Press, 1965), p. 759.

The Western Hero in the Dime Novel

Henry Nash Smith

I. THE DIME NOVEL HERO—FROM SETH JONES TO DEADWOOD DICK

In 1858 Erastus Beadle, a native of [James Fenimore] Cooper's country near Lake Otsego who had become a successful publisher in Buffalo, moved to New York in order to launch an ambitious project of cheap publishing for a mass audience. When a number of his song books and handbooks priced at ten cents made an immediate hit, he was encouraged to begin a weekly series of orange-backed "Dime Novels." The first of these appeared in June, 1860. It was followed by more than three hundred tales in the original series, and in due course by thousands of similar titles in more than thirty distinct series issued over a period of three decades. . . .

Beadle's editor was Orville J. Victor, a former newspaperman from Sandusky, Ohio, who supervised the production of dime novels and other series for thirty years. The distribution of the tales was handled at first through jobbers, but after 1864 by the American News Company, which was closely affiliated with the firm of Beadle & Adams. The usual print order for a dime novel was sixty thousand, but many titles were reprinted again and again. Edward S. Ellis's *Seth Jones,* which appeared as No. 8 of the original series, eventually sold more than four hundred thousand copies. Beadle's total sales between 1860 and 1865 approached five millions. These figures are not sensational by modern standards but they mark a revolution in nineteenth-century American publishing. An audience for fiction had been discovered that had not previously been known to exist. Beadle has some claim to rank among the industrial giants of his day. In his field, as an organizer and promoter of a basic discovery made by his predecessors, he was a figure comparable to Rockefeller or Carnegie.

Large-scale production implies regularity of output. The customer must be able to recognize the manufacturer's product by its uniform packaging—hence the various series with their characteristic formats. But a standard label is not enough; the product itself must be uniform and dependable. Victor's contribution to Beadle's success was the perfection of formulas which could be used by any number of writers, and the inspired alteration of these formulas according to the changing demands of the market. . . .

Writers on Victor's staff composed at great speed and in unbelievable quantity; many of them could turn out a thousand words an hour for twelve

Reprinted by permission of the publishers from pp. 90-92, 99-104, and 105-111 of Henry Nash Smith, **Virgin Land: The American West as Symbol and Myth** (Cambridge, Mass.: Harvard University Press). Copyright © 1950, by the President and Fellows of Harvard College.

hours at a stretch. Prentiss Ingraham . . . produced more than six hundred novels, besides plays and short stores. He is said to have written a thirty-five-thousand-word tale on one occasion in a day and a night. Fiction produced in these circumstances virtually takes on the character of automatic writing. The unabashed and systematic use of formulas strips from the writing every vestige of the interest usually sought in works of the imagination; it is entirely sub-literary. On the other hand, such work tends to become an objectified mass dream, like the moving pictures, the soap operas, or the comic books that are the present-day equivalents of the Beadle stories. The individual writer abandons his own personality and identifies himself with the reveries of his readers. It is the presumably close fidelity of the Beadle stories to the dream life of a vast inarticulate public that renders them valuable to the social historian and the historian of ideas.

Eventually, however, the industrial revolution in publishing leads to more and more frenzied competition among producers, and destroys even this value in the dime novel. Orville Victor said that when rival publishers entered the field the Beadle writers merely had to kill a few more Indians. But it went farther than that. The outworn formulas had to be given zest by a constant search after novel sensations. Circus tricks of horsemanship, incredible feats of shooting, more and more elaborate costumes, masks, and passwords were introduced, and even such ludicrous ornaments as worshippers of a Sun God devoted to human sacrifice in a vast underground cavern in the region of Yellowstone Park. Killing a few more Indians meant, in practice, exaggerating violence and bloodshed for their own sakes, to the point of an overt sadism. By the 1890s the Western dime novel had come to hinge almost entirely upon conflicts between detectives and bands of robbers that had little to do with the ostensibly Western locales. . . .

Toward 1880 Edward L. Wheeler created a character who despite the author's lack of imaginative coherence was impressive enough to deserve a place in the short roster of distinctive Western heroes. Wheeler's character bore the name Deadwood Dick, derived from the mining town which sprang up with the gold rush to the Black Hills in Dakota Territory, in the middle 1870s. Later Deadwood Dick operated throughout the West, although a certain fondness for mining camps reminds the reader of his origins. . . .

The most important traits of Deadwood Dick are that he too is without the upper-class rank that belongs exclusively to Easterners or Englishmen; that he possesses to a high degree such characteristic skills as riding and shooting; and that at the same time he is eligible for romantic attachments. Indeed, his life is cluttered with beautiful women pining for his love. . . . Overcoming his enemies by his own efforts and courage, he embodies the popular ideal of the self-made man. Such a hero, presumably humble in his origins and without formal education or inherited wealth, "confirmed Americans in the traditional belief that obstacles were to be overcome by the courageous, virile, and determined stand of the individual as an individual." Deadwood Dick, in fact, has achieved fortune as well as fame; he has an income of five thousand dollars a year from mining properties.

But after these simple points of departure have been established, the case of Deadwood Dick grows very complex. His amours are hopelessly confused. He has been married several times: one recorded wife sells herself to the devil and becomes unfaithful to him, another is killed, he is menaced by lovesick female villains, he fruitlessly courts Calamity Jane, he is subsequently the object of her hopeless devotion, and in the end he marries her. Furthermore, he shows traces not only of the Leatherstocking *persona* and of the traditional genteel hero, but likewise of the traditional villain: we learn that he has formerly been a bandit and on at least one occasion he reverts to banditry, in consequence of his wife's infidelity. Although he began life as a stage driver, in the dime novels considered here, he figures usually as a detective. And there are disquieting hints that at bottom he is a culture-hero of the Orpheus-Heracles type, for after being hanged as a bandit, as he remarks, "I was cut down and resuscitated by a friend, and thus, while I hung and paid my debt to nature and justice, I came back to life a free man whom no law in the universe could molest for past offenses." This Proteus claiming to be both immaculate and immortal has yet a further function: he exhibits a concern with social problems that is, as far as my knowledge extends, unique in the dime novels. In the avatar of "Deadwood Dick, Jr.," a character indistinguishable from Deadwood Dick, Sr., whom Wheeler apparently introduced in an effort to escape from overcomplications of plot, the hero leads a miners' union and as superintendent of a mine raises wages. He is, however, no socialist; he bitterly opposes an organization called the Lion Legion which is trying to seize the mine and operate it "on the commonweal plan." And on a visit to Chicago soon after the Haymarket Riots of 1886, Deadwood Dick, Jr., denounces the anarchists who are on trial because they are an undesirable foreign element. He declares that all the accused persons deserved to be hanged.

It may be that Deadwood Dick's appeal to readers of the Beadle novels depended on Wheeler's eclecticism, the device of ascribing to the hero all the skills, functions, graces, and successes that had ever fallen to the lot of any Western character, plus other powers derived from folk heroes of a forgotten past, and still other accomplishments prophetic of the coming reign of the dime novel detectives, Old Sleuth and Old Cap Collier. Deadwood Dick is certainly not an integrated construction of the imagination, and his fame reflects the kind of sensationalism that increased so markedly in the later 1870s.

II. BUFFALO BILL AND BUCK TAYLOR

The literary character of Buffalo Bill, most famous of dime novel heroes, is in many respects similar to that of Deadwood Dick. As the central figure of a long series of tales (more than two hundred by Prentiss Ingraham alone were still in print in the 1920s) Buffalo Bill performs exploits at least as various and as prodigious as those of his rival. Atlhough he is not so deeply involved with women as Deadwood Dick, he is young, handsome, well-tailored in a spectacular Western mode, and adept at all manly arts. In the 1890s he sometimes takes over Deadwood Dick's role of detective. The Buffalo Bill of literature, however, presents a different problem from that of Deadwood Dick because he was supposed to have as his original an actual man, the Honorable William F. Cody, former member of the Nebraska Legislature, who was constantly and flamboyantly in the public eye as principal actor in his Wild West show. It is true that a pretended original of Deadwood Dick, one Richard Clark, the first stage driver into Deadwood, has been mentioned by the scholiasts, but the man was too inconspicuous to be compared for an instant with the world-famous Cody, and Wheeler makes nothing of a possible factual basis for his character. On the other hand, the authors of the dime novels about Buffalo Bill constantly stress their claim to be writing chapters in the biography of a living celebrity.

This fact gives a special character to the Buffalo Bill of literature. From the time of Daniel Boone, the popular imagination had constantly transformed the facts of the westward movement in accordance with the requirements of myth. Boone himself lived to resent the popular image of him as an anarchic fugitive from civilization, and successive biographers tried in vain to correct what they considered a libelous distortion of the hero's real character. Davy Crockett of Tennessee, made the hero of a quite different cycle of Southwestern humor, was likewise completely transformed.

The literary development of the Wild Western hero in the second half of the nineteenth century made the divergence between fact and fiction even greater. Where Kit Carson had been represented as slaying his hundreds of Indians, the dime novel hero slew his thousands, with one hand tied behind him. But the *persona* created by the writers of popular fiction was so accurate an expression of the demands of the popular imagination that it proved powerful enough to shape an actual man in its own image. At the age of twenty-three Cody was a young plainsman like hundreds of others who had grown up beyond the Missouri. He had learned to make a living in the ways dictated by his environment—bull-whacking, serving as "office boy on horseback" for Alexander Majors of the famous overland freighting firm of Russel & Majors, driving stagecoaches, and scouting with detachments of troops fighting the plains Indians. His title of Buffalo Bill he had earned by hunting buffalo to feed construction crews of the Kansas Pacific Railroad. His actual life on the plains before he became a figure of the theater is almost completely obscured by the marvelous tales circulated later by talented press agents, but he does not seem to have been more skillful or daring than many of his companions. It was an accident, plus a natural gift for dramatizing himself, that made him the most highly publicized figure in all the history of the Wild West.

The accident was Cody's first meeting with Edward Z. C. Judson, alias Ned Buntline, the patriarch of blood-and-thunder romancers. Beginning as a contributor to Lewis Gaylord Clark's *Knickerbocker Magazine* in the late 1830s, Buntline had poured forth for decades an endless stream of sea stories, articles about field sports, tales of the Mexican War, temperance tracts, and Know-Nothing attacks on foreigners. By the time of his death in 1886 he had written more than two hundred stories of the dime novel type. In 1869 he signed a contract to write exclusively for the *New York Weekly,* published by Francis S. Street and Francis S. Smith; his fee was said to be $20,000 a year. Although Buntline's specialty had been sea stories, he evidently decided that it was time to turn systematically to the plains for materials: the nation at large was discovering the West. The editors of the *New York Weekly* announced that he had been traveling for two years in order to prepare himself to write a new series of works.

Buntline had heard of Major Frank North, commander of three companies of Pawnee scouts who had been enlisted in the regular army to fight the Sioux, and late in 1869 sought out North at Fort McPherson, Nebraska, with the intention of making him into a dime novel hero. But North declined. "If you want a man to fill that bill," he said, according to Cody's biographer Richard J. Walsh, "he's over there under the wagon." The man sleeping under the wagon was Cody, then a relatively obscure scout attached to North's command. Buntline talked with him, accompanied the Pawnees on a scouting expedition, and bestrode Cody's horse Powder Face. Then he went back to New York and introduced an apotheosized Cody to the readers of the *New York Weekly* in a serial entitled "Buffalo Bill, the King of the Border Men," which the editors characterized as "The Greatest Romance of the Age!" The story was subsequently brought out in book form, was reprinted again and again, and was still being sold by Sears, Roebuck at twenty-two cents in 1928. . . .

Buntline and the editors of the *New York Weekly* publicized Buffalo Bill so enthusiastically that he became something of a fad. James Gordon Bennett, editor of the *New York Herald,* who had been on one of General Sheridan's hunting trips for which Cody served as guide and had written him up lavishly as "the beau ideal of the plains," invited him to visit New York, and Sheridan encouraged Cody to make the trip. Buntline may well have planned the visit for purposes of his own; it coincided with the opening of a play *Buffalo Bill, the King of Bordermen* written by Fred G. Maeder on the basis of Buntline's serial in the *New York Weekly.* The scout was guest of honor at dinners given by Bennett and by August Belmont, although because of drink or naiveté he failed to appear at the Belmont dinner. On the evening of February 20, 1872, Buntline took him to the Bowery Theater to see the play. The climax, in the third act, was a hand-to-hand fight between Buffalo Bill and Jake McCanles in which they used knives reported to be three feet long, and in the stage version Bill married the Irish serving girl. The spotlight was turned on Cody and he was introduced to the audience. Later the manager of the theater offered him five hundred dollars a week to enact himself in the play. But Cody was too timid to accept the offer.

Nevertheless, he had not heard the last of Buntline, who continued writing to him at intervals urging him to come back East and go on the stage. At last Cody agreed to meet the novelist in Chicago, bringing his friend Texas Jack

Omohundro and twenty Indians. When they arrived, December 12, 1872, they had forgotten the Indians but Buntline hired supers and with his sublime nonchalance set about writing a script. In four hours he produced a piece "The Scouts of the Plains" that consisted mainly of shooting Indians, and the play opened four days later. Buntline, who had wisely arranged to be on the stage himself most of the time, managed to improvise a rambling conversation when his two scouts forgot all their lines. Then there was a great deal of shooting and the curtain came down. After three years of association with Buntline, Cody and Omohundro organized their own show, with John M. Burke as press agent and business manager, and Buffalo Bill was on his way to world-wide fame.

To Burke, apparently, belongs the credit for carrying through the major revision of the character of Buffalo Bill as Buntline had originally conceived it. Buntline had been content to exploit the rudimentary values of Indian fighting and stock romance; even the publicity writers for the *New York Weekly* had not claimed that Buffalo Bill was anything more than "the most daring scout, the best horseman, the best informed guide, and the greatest hunter of the present day." But Burke determined to enlarge the frame within which his client was to be viewed by the public. Buffalo Bill was to become an epic hero laden with the enormous weight of universal history. He was to be placed beside Boone and Frémont and Carson in the roster of American heroes, and like them was to be interpreted as a pioneer of civilization and a standard bearer of progress, although of course no showman would forget the box-office appeal of black powder and trick riding. This conception Burke dinned into Cody's ears so constantly that the hero himself took up the clichés, and in his old age used to say, "I stood between savagery and civilization most all my early days." The actual phrasing of the slogan may have been due to Prentiss Ingraham, the dime novelist, who had become virtually a staff writer for Cody by 1878, and possibly earlier. Ingraham wrote that Buffalo Bill was

> one of America's strange heroes who has loved the trackless wilds, rolling plains and mountain solitudes of our land, far more than the bustle and turmoil, the busy life and joys of our cities, and who has stood as a barrier between civilization and savagery, risking his own life to save the lives of others.

Ingraham composed the play that Cody used during the season 1878-1879, and presumably also the "autobiography" published in 1879. It will be recalled that before his death in 1904, he produced more than two hundred stories about Buffalo Bill, in addition to his probable authorship of a large number of dime novels signed by Cody.

From his earliest youth Ingraham's Buffalo Bill is associated with the spectral apparitions, the chain-mail shirts that can stop bullets, and the beautiful transvested maidens seeking revenge that are normal in the later dime novels. The novelist's personal idiosyncrasy—which Cody's own tastes encouraged—was his delight in splendor of attire. The costume which he designed for Buffalo

Bill's first appearance as a Pony Express Rider in the tale *Gold Plume, the Boy Bandit* was described as

> a red velvet jacket, white corduroy pants, stuck in handsome top boots, which were armed with heavy gold spurs, and . . . upon his head a gray sombrero, encircled by a gold cord and looped up on the left side with a pin representing a spur.
>
> He also wore an embroidered silk shirt, a black cravat, gauntlet gloves, and a sash of red silk, in which were stuck a pair of revolvers and a dirk-knife.

In his autobiography Cody—or Ingraham—describes a costume which the hunter wore when he acted as guide for Sheridan, Bennett, and other celebrities. He says that since "it was a nobby and high-toned outfit," he determined to put on a little style himself.

> So I dressed in a new suit of light buckskin, trimmed along the seams with fringes of the same material; and I put on a crimson shirt handsomely ornamented on the bosom, while on my head I wore a broad *sombrero*. Then mounting a snowy white horse—a gallant stepper—I rode down from the fort to the camp, rifle in hand. I felt first-rate that morning, and looked well.

Several years later, in the summer of 1876, when Cody fought his much publicized duel with Yellow Hand and took "the first scalp for Custer" under the eyes of newspaper correspondents, he wore a costume that must have been taken from the wardrobe of his theatrical company. It consisted of a Mexican suit of black velvet, slashed with scarlet and trimmed with silver buttons and lace. These costumes, fictional and actual, illustrate the blending of Cody with his theatrical role to the point where no one—least of all the man himself—could say where the actual left off and where dime novel fiction began.

As if to exhaust all the possible relationships between fact and imagination, Cody's press-agents caused many stories to be issued under his own name. Although he himself does not figure in the plots of these stories, they closely resemble those in which he does. *Deadly-Eye,* issued with *The Prairie Rover* in 1875 in the short-lived Beadle & Adams 20 Cent Novel series, relates the exploits of the Unknown Scout, alias Deadly-Eye, alias Alfred Carleton, young, handsome, and of such sartorial splendor that the story must be by Ingraham. Like the young Buffalo Bill in Buntline's first story, the Unknown Scout is motivated by a thirst for vengeance upon the slayer of his parents. Since he has been educated in the East and speaks the straight rhetoric of the genteel hero, the Unknown Scout represents the Seth Jones use of the *persona* as a disguise and can marry the heroine Sibyl Conrad without impediments. Gold Spurs, hero of *Gold Bullet Sport; or, The Knight of the Overland,* is even more elegant than the Unknown Scout; he has a velvet jacket and gold-plated spurs and weapons that again strongly suggest Ingraham's authorship. He is assisted by a benign hunter and trapper named Buckskin Ben who speaks in dialect and is viewed with the patronizing approval traditionally reserved for replicas of Leatherstocking. Since the Gold Bullet Sport wears many disguises in the course of his pursuit of the villain, and is represented as having served a prison term after a false conviction of bank robbery, he has some of the criminal flavor that clings to Deadwood Dick. In view of these similarities one is not surprised to find the Buffalo Bill of later Ingraham stories appearing as a detective and as a stage driver. And one recalls that the Deadwood Coach was always a part of Buffalo Bill's Wild West show.

The Wild Western hero as a cowboy, who in the twentieth century has become the dominant type, first appeared in the wake of Buffalo Bill in the late 1880s. American readers of the national magazines had long been familiar with Mexican *rancheros* and *vaqueros* in California and Texas, but the American hired man on horseback did not become a celebrated figure until the range industry spread northward from Texas over the Great Plains in the early 1870s. In this decade the term "herder" was as likely to be used as the classic name of "cowboy," and it usually called up the image of a semibarbarous laborer who lived a dull, monotonous life of hard fare and poor shelter. Laura Winthrop Johnson, writing for Lippincott's in 1875, saw no glamor in the "rough men with shaggy hair and wild, staring eyes, in butternut trousers stuffed into great rough boots" whom she described at a round-up in Wyoming.

Toward the end of the decade, however, Henry King, a writer for *Scribner's,* was able to detect a touch of the picturesque in the ranch life of western Kansas. Although he was depressed by the bleak solitude of the plains, he enjoyed the exotic note of color introduced by the costumes of the herdsmen, who affected "old Castilian sombreros, and open-legged trowsers with rows of buttons, and jackets gaudy with many-colored braid and Indian beads, and now and then a blood-red scarf like a matador's." King also suggested that the cowboy had some virtues despite his violence: he was generous, brave, and scrupulously honest, with "a strange, paradoxical code of personal honor, in vindication of which he will obtrude his life as though it were but a toy." As late as 1881, however, the pejorative connotations of the term "cowboy" were still uppermost. President Chester A. Arthur's First Annual Message to Congress mentioned a disturbance of the public tranquility by a band of "armed desperadoes known as 'Cowboys,' probably numbering from fifty to one hundred men," who had for months been committing acts of lawlessness and brutality in the Territory of Arizona, and across the border in Mexico. He asked for legislation empowering the Army to intervene.

But the Western point of view was different. In 1882 the citizens of North Platte, Nebraska, decided to organize a big Fourth of July celebration, an "Old Glory blowout," that would resemble what we know as a rodeo. Cody, who was already a famous theatrical figure and had bought a ranch in the vicinity, was appointed Grand Marshal. Thus was the Wild West show born. Since North Platte was in cattle country, the roping and riding and shooting contests dominated the celebration and determined the character of the show which Cody took on the road next year. His brightest cowboy star was Buck Taylor, who could ride the worst bucking horse, throw a steer by the horns or tail, and pick up a neckerchief from the ground at full speed.

Probably the earliest use of a cowboy hero in the Beadle novels is an alleged biography of Taylor by Prentiss Ingraham published in 1887. In this narrative, Taylor comes as a youngster to a camp of Captain McNally's Texas Rangers, and asks to be enlisted. After his prowess as a pugilist and as a bronco rider has been tested, he is admitted to the chosen band. The principal activity of the Rangers is fighting Mexican raiders headed by one Rafael, but Taylor identifies himself with the tradition of Leatherstocking when he is captured by Comanches and freed by an Indian he has befriended, as well as when he rescues McNally's daughter from the Indians. The Rangers likewise wear a costume that belongs to the tradition—leggings and hunting coats—although they have adopted the broad sombreros of Mexican culture. But Ingraham soon designed a more adequate costume for Buck Taylor, one equal to the splendor of Buffalo Bill:

> He was dressed in somewhat gaudy attire, wore a watch and chain, diamond pin in his black scarf, representing a miniature spur, and upon the small finger of his right hand there was a ring, the design being a horseshoe of rubies.
>
> About his broad-brimmed, dove-colored sombrero was coiled a miniature lariat [*sic*], so that the spur, horseshoe and lasso designated his calling.

As a press agent for the Wild West show Ingraham strove to offset the bad reputation which cowboys had with the public. In *The Cowboy Clan; or, The Tigress of Texas. A Romance of Buck Taylor and his Boys in Buckskin* he undertakes a defense of the cowboys as a class. They are indeed reckless, but light-hearted, fearless, generous, and "noble in their treatment of a friend or a fallen foe." They are feared by Indians and evil-doers but admired and respected by soldiers and people of the settlements. Surgeon Hassam, of the Medical Corps of the Army, continues this defense in another story by Ingraham. Because the cowboys are a little wild, he tells Buck, they are terribly maligned by those who do not know them. Taylor agrees. "I know well," he adds, "that a great many wicked men have crept into the ranks of our cowboy bands; but there are plenty of them who are true as steel and honest as they can be." His note is somewhat plaintive: "We lead a wild life, get hard knocks, rough usage and our lives are in constant peril, and the settling of a difficulty is an appeal to revolver or knife; but after all we are not as black as we are painted."

Whatever may be the merits of the dime novel cowboy, however, he apparently has nothing to do with cattle. If an occasional story (like Philip S. Warne's *Lariat Lil; or, The Cast for a Life. A Story of Love and Jealousy*) describes the actual business of a round-up, most cowboy tales are hardly distinguishable from the Deadwood Dick and Buffalo Bill series. The professional duty of Beadle cowboys is to fight Indians, Mexicans, and outlaws. And the atmosphere created by wronged women seeking vengeance upon their false lovers, Mexican girls in men's clothing, and Army officers detailed for secret service is thoroughly typical of the decadent phase of Beadle fiction. The introduction of characters described as cowboys is little more than an effort to achieve an air of contemporaneity. It does not change the shape of Wild Western fiction.

Roosevelt, Remington, Wister: Consensus and the West

G. Edward White

"In 1885," Owen Wister wrote in the preface of his fifth volume of western stories,

> the Eastern notion of the West was "Alkali Ike" and smoking pistols. No kind of serious art had presented the frontier as yet. . . . Then, Mr. Roosevelt began to publish his vivid, robust accounts of Montana life. But words alone, no matter how skillfully used, were not of themselves adequate to present to the public a picture so strange and new. Another art was needed, and most luckily the man with the seeing eye and shaping hand arrived. A monument to Frederic Remington will undoubtedly rise some day; the artist who more than any one has gathered up in a grand grasp an entire era of this country's history, and handed it down visible, living, picturesque, for coming generations to see.

Roosevelt, Remington, and his humble self, Wister felt, had produced the kind of serious response to the West which had helped to transform it, for his eastern friends, from a borderland of savagery and civilization to "an entire era of this country's history."

The western theme as expressed by Wister and his colleagues bears only a slight resemblance to earlier eastern views, which focus on those aspects of the western experience that seemed in opposition to the social order. The strength of the Leatherstocking Tales, for example, lies in the attractiveness of Natty Bumppo's anarchism, which his abundant natural environment reinforces, but Roosevelt, Remington, and Wister picture the West not as an alternative to civilization but as a particular kind of civilization, a "grim, harsh land," filled with "men with the bark on," where "a man must take care of himself." Rather than drawing distinctions between the presence and absence of organized society, they distinguish between two types of social orders—one agrarian, rural, egalitarian, and ethnically and racially homogeneous (West), and the other industrial, urban, elitist, ethnically heterogeneous, and racially mixed (East). Since they view life in the West within the wide-ranging, fluctuating, and elusive social context of late nineteenth- and early twentieth-century America, they adopt a more "serious" and detailed approach than [James Fenimore] Cooper, [Washington] Irving, and [Francis] Parkman.

Roosevelt, Remington, and Wister gave careful attention to the hates, dreams, and misfortunes of Westerners as well as to their values and prejudices, because each of them sensed that to come to grips with the western experience was to encounter certain aspects of American culture which the rush of industrialism threatened to sweep away. They were motivated to "westernize" themselves, in a way that earlier writers and tourists were not, by their individual dissatisfactions with their eastern heritage. Each sought for something in the West with which he could identify, and that search lent his experiences a greater significance. Idiosyncratic as their searches were, however, they can be seen to have a common cultural foundation in the state of economic and social flux that marked the latter portions of the nineteenth century. . . .

Eventually individuals of Remington's and Wister's generation attempted to turn, like prodigal sons, to their fathers for security and guidance. In some cases this reassertion of a rural, egalitarian, Anglo-Saxon heritage took the form of wistful attempts to replace industrial society with an agrarian-based utopia; in others it manifested itself in a neo-Jacksonian indictment of the "undemocratic" corporation; in still others it burst out in patriotism, xenophobia, and racism. . . .

The "Wild" West came, in this view, to represent the stage of civilization in America before the advent of industrialization, and as such it was both romantic and potentially tragic. Its virtues (self-reliance, "hardiness," and the like) were heroic because they suggested to Easterners of Roosevelt's generation the glories of their past, while harmonizing with their present aspirations. Yet the western kind of rugged individualism was threatened by the march of technological progress, and Remington's and Wister's contemporaries were excessively aware of the dire future in store for that America once the armies from the East reached its borders.

As the nineteenth century drew to a close and the problems of urban living became more complicated, Easterners turned with increasing attentiveness to the writings of those individualists who had encountered the western experience. After 1885, as Wister said, art of the frontier became increasingly serious business. Contemporary criticism of Roosevelt, Remington, and Wister emphasized more and more the relevance of a western way of life to eastern Americans. Though early reviews often reflect the older eastern conception of the West as a wilderness filled with strange inhabitants, as the nineteenth century moves toward its conclusion, that attitude is increasingly accompanied by a sense that the West may symbolize the last stages of preindustrial America, about to pass into oblivion. Twentieth-century reviews have entirely dropped the notion of the West as a strange wilderness and emphasize its historic and "American" qualities.

Accompanying this change in attitude toward the region is a differing response to the writers themselves.. Early reviewers tend to picture Roosevelt, Remington, and Wister as chroniclers of strange happenings. As the image of the West takes on a more historic quality, the trio of writers is seen as commentators on a dying civilization, historians of America. And finally, as the spirit of the West becomes infused with other attempts to reassert American traditions in the decade of consensus, Roosevelt, Remington, and Wister are seen as patriotic-spirited "good Americans." . . .

"Wilderness" and "strange" are words often used to describe the West in the early reviews of Roosevelt's work, coupled with "savage" and "barbarous" to denote such western inhabitants as the cowboy, and "practical" and "experienced" to characterize Roosevelt. . . .

The image of "young gentlemen" going West on a lark implies a conception of the West as an uncivilized wasteland, fit for a "gilded" youth's momentary indulgences. The characterization of the cowboys as rough, crude, and reckless harmonizes with Parkman's portraits of coarse trappers and Irving's description of sinister backwoodsmen. Consistent with these attitudes is the picturing of Roosevelt as one who "has both felt the delights and the troubles of a free, independent life." For the most part, the West remained in these reviews simply a region void of civilization, with the pleasures and pains which accompanied society's absence.

Almost simultaneously with the closing of the frontier in 1891 and the publication of the Turner thesis two years later, however, came a slight shift in attitude—a sense that whatever peculiar characteristics life on the "border-land of civilization" took, that life was passing from view and, as such, had begun to take on a historical importance that required closer study. . . .

The New York *Times,* which in 1893 expressed pleasure at Roosevelt's portrait of "that part of the United States, though relatively small, which is still a wilderness," reversed its field as civilization threatened to render the Old West obsolete. In 1894 it chided those "rather aristocratic dwellers on the Atlantic coast" who deemed in earlier times "frontier people as somewhat akin to barbarians"; lamented that "there is even to-day, in large cities, a population prone to regard the remote West in the same light"; and called the West "an integral part of the mighty American Republic." In 1896, in a review of Roosevelt's *Ranch Life and the Hunting Trail,* the *Times* noted that "if the cattle country of the West is fast being curtailed . . . the greater, then, must be the interest felt in the nomadic, or pastoral conditions of former years." Roosevelt's cowboy has evolved in these reviews from a "pretty rough character" to a "rational, understandable human being," and from a reckless fatalist who "earned wages laboriously, and spent them foolishly" to a "strong, self-reliant, and manly" individual with "many estimable traits." . . .

In his ultimate role Roosevelt was lauded by *Forum* in 1896 for his "noble and patriotic" *Winning of the West.* In a lengthy review which set the tone for forthcoming paeans to the Rough Riders, *Forum* thanked Roosevelt for "a history that enlarges . . . comprehension of the character of the nation . . . by unfolding . . . the heroic and noble deeds of the generations that have preceded." "Roosevelt," the review continued, "has seen that the history of the West is the history of the movement of a people which cannot be understood except in connection with the similar movements that have characterized the Aryan race, and especially the English portion of it . . . Mr. Roosevelt is never weary of pointing out to us the part the West has played in making the American nation what it is. . . . He is a man and an American, and nothing that is human and American is alien to him."

Roosevelt as superpatriot captured the imagination of many eastern reviewers after 1898, and his image as a man of the West became increasingly identified with his "Americanism." He became the supreme Rough Rider, the foremost member of that regiment of true Americans. . . .

As early as 1893, the sense of the West as manly, egalitarian, self-reliant, and Aryan, and thus the focus of true America, had been expressed in scholarly form by Frederick Jackson Turner in his "Significance of the Frontier." In a letter to Turner a year later, Roosevelt said that he thought the "pamphlet on the Frontier . . . struck some first class ideas" and "put into definite shape a good deal of thought which has been floating around rather loosely"; he added in an 1896 letter to Turner, "I think it will be a good thing for this country when the West, as it used to be called, the Centre, as it really is, grows so big that it can no more be jealous of the East." And in those instances when the ex-ranchman was not overly eager to connect his western experiences to the glories of the American past, his reviewers often helped him out. "Self-reliance" may have had a personal meaning to Roosevelt in Dakota, but to the *Nation* it was one of those traits associated with "the development of the country."

Remington's western writings appeared a full decade later than Roosevelt's first effort, and hence few reviewers used the term "wilderness" to characterize the West of *Pony Tracks* and *Crooked Trails.* However, the New York *Tribune* for 1895 noted that "the pony tracks led us into many strange and stirring scenes." The *Bookman* in the same year commented on "the vigour and occasional crudeness of the better class of people to be met in the West" and called Remington's experiences "strange and adventurous." . . .

By 1898 reviewers had made a clear connection between Remington's work and the passing of a phase of America. The *Dial* called Remington "the delineator par excellence of the Indian, the cowboy and the greaser" and felt that "the sharp realism of his pictures will make them of positive historical value to future generations, when the types and phases of American character he chooses to portray have disappeared from the shifting stage of our national life." The *Times* noted that "the city and town-confined man who reads this book will marvel at the life Mr. Remington spreads out before him," pointing out that "the stories recall days now largely passed . . . which still live and find a welcome place in story."

In the midst of the decade of consensus Remington's *John Ermine of the*

Yellowstone exhibited his hatred of the "cards and custards" of eastern civilization by demonstrating the selfishness and hypocrisy of the attitudes of white characters toward his Indianized hero. At the close of the novel John Ermine is pictured as a victim of the "march of white humanity" across the western plains: the white soldiers are particularly anxious to initiate Ermine into their community, take his hair out of braids, and teach him army phrases, but the moment he does not conform to his "station" and aspires after Katherine Searles they reject him and eventually attempt to kill him. Reviewers, with their own general commitment to white supremacy and worship of the Anglo-Saxon tradition, were baffled by Remington's tragedy. . . .

The *Lamp*, in a 1903 review of *John Ermine*, [commented] . . . "When at a critical period [Ermine] comes under the influence of a mysterious hermit who works purposely upon the white nature of his pupil, . . . one . . . concludes that the situation is being reasonably unfolded and that the all-conquering Anglo-Saxon blood will assume its place. . . . Here is the chance to efface early association and allow innate nobility, heroism, and devotion [to come through] ." "But," noted the *Lamp*, "the girl received John Ermine's homage as impertinence. In his humiliation white blood and heredity do not count. John Ermine is Indian, all Indian. . . . He dies practically a savage; his early training has won." The review called *John Ermine* "an interesting variant on the frontier novel" and labeled Remington "of stern stuff" for his sense of Ermine's social limitations. It could no more sense the indictment of white civilization in Ermine's tragedy than Remington himself could sense the inconsistency between this indictment and his own racist attitudes. . . .

Wister's image as a historian of the Old West was even more clearly associated with his patriotic qualities, in the minds of his readers, than that of Roosevelt or Remington. *World's Work*, in a review of the *Jimmyjohn Boss*, made a characteristic connection between the passing of Wister's West and the spirit of "real" America. "Wister," it wrote, "has exploited the essential spirit of frontier Wyoming and Arizona, the cattle people and the cattle country, with the plains and mountains where they lived, all wholly American of our blood and soil." In the same paragraph that it spoke of "cowboys and Indians and soldiers, and hard women of that lynch-law belt now gone," *World's Work* pointed out that "Mr. Wister's work expresses . . . what precious little other American fiction tries to express—Americanism." "To catch the deeper meaning of our life," the review concluded, "one's path must be toward that Western verge of the continent where all white men are American-born, because there only are the culture and conservatism of the East, the chivalry and the fire-eating spirit of the South, and the broad unhampered gambler's view of life native to raw Western soil, all transmuted into a democracy of no distinctions." . . .

In general, contemporary critics of *The Virginian* were quick to respond to the same heroic qualities that newspaper correspondents saw in the Rough Riders. Several reviews agreed with Mabie's conception of the Virginian as a real man: Hamblen Sears of the *Book Buyer*, for one, stated in 1902 that the horseman of the plains "is no pasteboard type to hang the rags of plot and passion on. . . . Mr. Wister knows how to set up his man on his own legs in all his lithe, tiger-like build." The Virginian was also gentlemanly ("Owen Wister's Virginian is a gentleman under a coat of roughness," noted the *Atlantic*), "American" ("genuinely patriotic without being maudlin," said the *Bookman*), and, of course, self-reliant (as *Forum* phrased it, "sure of his own mind and deed"). . . . In summation, Wister, in "setting forth a phase of life which is to be found only in the United States," and in giving artistic embodiment to "a species of man fast passing into a remembrance," had, for the New York *Times*—and doubtless many others—"come pretty near to writing the American novel."

Contemporary reaction to Remington, Roosevelt, and Wister in the late nineties and 1900s indicates the degree to which the Wild West had become firmly associated with the American heritage. Those aspects of the western experience that they emphasized struck vibrant chords in the hearts of their readers. As technological and financial triumphs, coupled with a vast increase in population of an increasingly mixed ethnic nature, made white Anglo-Saxon America, in the eyes of the native-born, both the glorious and most threatened nation in the world, the role of masculinity, individualism, and gentlemanliness became of crucial interest, and the fact that Roosevelt, Remington, and Wister examined such topics in a rapidly passing western context meant that both their writings and that context would be considered all the more significant. Thus the trio of writers took part in, as it were, a regional round-robin: their eastern heritage both drove them West and enabled them to respond to the western experience in such a way as to make it attractive to their eastern contemporaries, who came to envisage an integration of East and West in a twentieth-century America that contained the best of both.

That Wister, Remington, and Roosevelt, in this sense, came full cycle can be seen from their comments on one another as the turbulence of the nineties gave way to the illusory calm of the decade of consensus. In 1895 Roosevelt called Wister "a teller of tales of strong men" and suggested that he dealt with "the great problems of American existence and the infinite picturesqueness of our life as it has been and is being led here on our own continent." . . . And by 1907 Roosevelt could state about Remington what he had implied about Wister:

> I regard Frederic Remington as one of the Americans who has done real work for this country, and we all owe him a debt of gratitude. . . . It is no small thing for the nation that such an artist and man of letters should arise to make permanent record of certain of the most interesting features of our national life . . . [Remington] is, of course, one of the most typical American artists we have ever had, and he has portrayed a most characteristic and yet vanishing type of American life. The soldier, the cowboy and rancher, the Indian, the horses and the cattle of the plains, will live in his pictures and bronzes for all time.

Wister was equally enthusiastic about the contribution Roosevelt and

Remington had made to an understanding of the West in its American perspective. As early as 1891 he felt that "Roosevelt had seen the sagebrush true, and felt its poetry," and was a "pioneer in taking the cowboy seriously." In 1894 Wister wrote Roosevelt that he liked the "manliness and simplicity" of *The Wilderness Hunter,* and in 1895 he congratulated Roosevelt on his *American Ideals,* which one critic called a mass of "braggadocio and condescension." . . . On Remington, Wister surpassed himself. . . . "When Remington came with only a pencil, I forgot the rest. . . . No words of mine can tell you how Remington has been a poet here." And by 1902, Wister's "American heart" was smote all the more with the indigenous qualities of Remington's work. "Remington has taken the likeness of the modern American soldier," he wrote, "and stamped it upon our minds with a blow as clean-cut as is the impression of the American eagle upon our coins in the mint. . . . Remington is drawing the most picturesque of the American people. . . . Remington is not merely an artist; he is a national treasure."

Even the misanthropic Remington could occasionally stir himself to praise his western colleagues. In 1899 he wrote to Wister: "You have an air tight cinch on the West—others may monkey but you arrive with a horrible crash every pop"; and he sent back one of Wister's stories for *Harper's* in 1900 with the notation: "It doesn't need illustrating—it's all there—I wouldn't want to interfere." . . .

Ultimately, even Roosevelt, Remington, and Wister, who had formed friendships with one another early in life and solidified them as each became famous, fell increasingly into conventionalized nostalgic and patriotic prose to characterize themselves and one another as the twentieth century advanced. Besides dusting off their noblest and most chauvinistic phrases to describe each other, the trio identified themselves as "good Americans." "It would be a mistake to nominate me for President," Roosevelt noted in 1916, "unless the country has as its mood something of the heroic." "They say my writings are very American," wrote Wister in 1908. "They ought to be. I have been on this soil, ancestrally speaking, since the Merion settlement in Pennsylvania, more than two hundred years." "I hated Europe," with its "collars, cuffs and foreign languages," Remington confessed to Perriton Maxwell in 1907, to which Maxwell responded: "[Remington's] has always been a praiseworthy egotism. He is proud of his Americanism."

As critic after critic sang *The Virginian's* praises, spoke of the Americanness of Roosevelt and Remington, and reveled in the fond memories of the western experience, the decade of consensus came to agree with Wister that the West was "the poetic episode most deeply native we possess." As such the cowboy took his place in a long line of inspiringly anarchistic American heroes, cartoonists reminded the public that a former Rough Rider occupied the White House, and Remington "immortalized himself" in bronze and silently counted his $25,000 a year salary. In their extraordinary desire to retain a piece of the past in a world oriented toward some frightfully technological future, Americans of the 1900s tried to balance their awareness of the implications of a complex industrial society with their hopes that that society might not turn out to be so complicated. . . .

The West that the trio had helped to implant in the American imagination was no more an oasis in the urban desert than its cowboy inhabitants were gentlemen, however, and older America eventually became a feeble patriarch as the solid framework of principles and attitudes which had buttressed the decade of consensus rotted and crumbled. Morality, in its testy old age, appeared as prudery; the gentleman's world of Anglo-Saxonism degenerated into squalling nationalism and xenophobia; the technocratic paternalists gave way to an administration which believed that "the business of government is business"; and small-town America became Main Street.

For those of the decade of consensus who survived, the times became increasingly painful. Remington, beleagured by civilization's advances, ate and drank himself to death. Roosevelt, almost blind and infirm, made a pitiful attempt to revive the spirit of his Rough Riders in a volunteer regiment in 1917 and found polite but firm rebuffs on all sides. And Wister, who felt himself an "old-timer" in 1910, suffered through the twenties, the depression, and the New Deal. In 1933 he declined an invitation to visit Wyoming, saying that "too many ghosts are there for me. . . . I don't want to see any of that country again. Too much nostalgic for past happenings." One of his obituaries in 1938 noted that "one turns in vain to a majority of American histories of literature to find him as much as mentioned; while even most of the exceptions do little more than comment glancingly in one sentence upon the *Virginian,* and nearly all but dismiss it as the relatively respectable ancestor of a whole host of widely romanticized cowboy fictions."

To modern eyes the numerous attempts to balance East and West in the 1890s and 1900s may seem as self-assured and contrived as the stiffest of Edwardian collars. Nevertheless, the search in America for an understanding of industrial and urban life, with its consequent countersearch for an alternative to that life, remains our irrevocable link to the generations of Roosevelt, Remington, and Wister. Countless commentators of the 1960s have investigated with great seriousness the task of eastern living, and countless Americans, in turn, have exhibited a strong attraction for fantasy versions of the Wild West, in the form of popular novels, motion pictures, and radio and television serials. The President of the United States in 1958 named Westerns as his favorite literary genre; in 1964 *The Virginian* appeared as a television series; and Remington's paintings still command impressive sums at urban art auctions.

It was the Roosevelt generation that first called attention to a dilemma in American culture which is still present: how to come to terms with metropolitan living while demonstrating the relevancy of alternative existences. The search for freedom from a corporate and technological world still manifests itself in the arena of national politics, as when in the flush of Barry Goldwater's triumph at the Republican Convention in 1964 pride-filled delegates rose to denounce the "Eastern Establishment," whose yoke they had momentarily cast off. Perhaps such attempts to resist the tide of corporate professionalism are as fallacious as earlier desires to implant the yeoman farmer in the midst of technocratic America, but they represent the same reluctance on the part of Americans to wholly embrace an urban and industrial society without positing alternatives to it.

The West As Fiction

Philip C. Durham and Everett L. Jones

[Before leaving this analysis of Western literature, we should examine one of its most overlooked consequences. From Part I it should be clear that the Western frontier was a multi-ethnic, multi-racial place. Virtually all of the literature cited in this section, however, indicates that the writers of Western tales chose to keep the range White and Anglo-Saxon. Authors Philip Durham and Everett Jones in their book, *The Negro Cowboys,* attempt to explain the reason for the absence of Blacks from Western literature, placing much of the blame on the influential Owen Wister.]

The trails end where fiction begins. As the records show, Negroes helped to open and hold the West. They explored the plains and mountains, fought Indians, dug gold and silver, and trapped wild horses and wolves. Some were outlaws and some were law officers. Thousands rode in the cavalry, and thousands more were cowboys. And for a while, at least, some performed in rodeos and others rode on many of the country's major race tracks.

Yet, Negroes rarely appear in Western fiction. They are not, for example, in the dime novels. Approximately two thirds of the 3,158 dime novels published by Beadle and Adams between 1860 and 1898 are laid in the trans-Mississippi West, where they deal with frontiersmen, desperadoes, miners and assorted Texas heroes and badmen. Negroes appear only insignificantly in their plots—action-packed stories far more concerned with bloodthirsty Indians, virtuous maidens, ferocious robbers and leering . . . villains than with cowhands and six guns. The dime novels were the predecessors, but not the progenitors, of the true Western story.

Today's Western story began in 1902 with the publication of Owen Wister's *The Virginian,* long after the great trail drives, years after barbed wire, railroads and improved cattle breeding methods had changed the West. Even in 1902 *The Virginian* was a novel about a man of the past, about a hero out of a

Reprinted by permission of Dodd, Mead & Company, Inc. from The Negro Cowboys by Philip C. Durham and Everett L. Jones. Copyright © 1965 by Philip C. Durham and Everett L. Jones.

heroic and idealized age. Wister's hero rode proudly through a nearly lawless Wyoming, making his own justice, hanging rustlers and outshooting the villain in scenes that were prototypes for thousands of similar scenes in later stories and motion pictures. But by 1902 that lawless Wyoming had already disappeared. It had ended, for all practical purposes, with the defeat of the cattlemen in the Johnson County War of 1892. The Wyoming of 1902 was still rough and occasionally bloody, but juries, judges and sheriffs dispensed justice. Had a real Virginian been living when the novel was published, he might well have been tried by a Wyoming jury and hanged by a Wyoming sheriff. Certainly that was the fate of Tom Horn, the "regulator" and hunter of rustlers who was hanged in 1903.

Even *The Virginian,* then, was essentially a historical novel, set in a West that was already a memory. It was better than many of its later imitations, for Owen Wister had visited the West as early as 1885 and had hunted and fished with many of the old-time cowmen and cowboys; and he had ridden hundreds of miles through Western country, recording conversations, anecdotes and descriptions of scenery in his journals. He had been, in a sense, one of the first of the Eastern dudes, finding the great, strange West a romantic and exciting spectacle. Many of the cattlemen and cowboys he met seemed like noble savages, exotic and colorful, uninhibited and a little shocking in their speech and action, but nature's noblemen. Years later he described them, sentimentalized and somewhat oversimplified, in *The Virginian.*

There were working Negro cowboys in the West that Wister visited, but there are none in his fiction. He probably saw comparatively few, for his journals show that his Western trips were vacations, essentially social visits or hunting and fishing trips. Just as there are cowboys, but few cows—and rustlers, but few calves or steers—in his stories, so there are few working cowboys of any kind in his journals. While the cowboys were roping, castrating, branding, fencing, driving or loading cattle, Wister was usually riding, hunting or fishing with a cattleman host or guide. He saw cowboys at leisure, but rarely at work.

Although his grandmother, Fanny Kemble, had written one of the greatest pre-Civil War protests against the institution of slavery, Owen Wister shared the racial prejudices of his time and social class. One of his few strong disagreements with his Harvard friend Theodore Roosevelt was caused by Roosevelt's appointment of a Negro to a minor federal post. Their correspondence is eloquent testimony of Wister's attitude toward Negroes. So, too, are occasional passages in Wister's stories and journals.

Yet *The Virginian* is not necessarily an anti-Negro book because it contains no Negro characters. What it expresses, rather, as does most of Wister's work, is an admiration for the Anglo-Saxon, for the conquering white man, for the noble Nordic. It is expressed, for example, in Wister's description of American cowboys in an article published in *Harper's* in 1895: " . . . they came in shoals— Saxon boys of picked courage (none but the plucky ones could survive) from South and North, from town and country." This admiration for the plucky white race was one that Wister shared with another author whom he greatly admired—Rudyard Kipling. It was, moreover, one that he shared with millions of his countrymen at the beginning of the twentieth century.

One cause of widespread pride in the peculiar virtues of the white race was rationalization of new United States imperialism. In 1900 Americans elected William McKinley and so endorsed a policy by which America would assume its share of "the white man's burden." In the same year, Congress enacted the Platt Amendment, which specifically claimed the right of the United States to interfere in Cuba to protect the liberty or property of American citizens. Puerto Rico had been occupied since the Spanish-American War. United States troops were fighting in the Philippine Islands against Filipinos who were continuing their revolution for independence. And in 1900, American troops were part of the relief expedition sent to suppress the Boxer Rebellion in China. Some of these activities were justified on simple grounds of economic advantage or military necessity, but all were defended on the grounds of white supremacy and of white moral responsibility for Christianizing and educating inferior and colored peoples. So the newspapers and magazines were full of praise of Anglo-Saxon law, Aryan civilization and the Nordic tradition of courage and chivalry. At the same time they preached the duty of defending the spiritual values of a white civilization from the menaces of the yellow peril or black savagery.

Almost inevitably this new exaltation of the Anglo-Saxon and the Aryan involved corresponding denigration of Negroes in America. The decade following 1900 has frequently been called the "nadir" of white-Negro relations in America. It was during this decade that opinions of "sociologists" like Frederick L. Hoffman gained wide currency: he wrote that "all facts prove that education, philanthropy, and religion have failed to develop [among the Negroes] higher appreciation of the stern and uncompromising virtues of the Aryan race." Many novels echoed and amplified this belief; perhaps the most successful of them was Thomas Dixon's *The Clansman* (1905), which later became the basis of the motion picture *The Birth of a Nation.* This novel, which glorified the Ku Klux Klan, described its emergence as "one of the most dramatic chapters in the history of the Aryan race." Both Dixon's message and his prose style are well illustrated by his description of the arrival of the invalided Thaddeus Stevens at the impeachment proceedings against President Johnson: "The negroes placed him in an arm-chair facing the semicircle of Senators, and crouched down on their haunches beside him. Their kinky heads, black skin, thick lips, white teeth, and flat noses made for the moment a curious symbolic frame for the chalk-white passion of the old Commoner's face.

"No sculptor ever dreamed a more sinister emblem of the corruption of a race of empire-builders than this group. Its black figures, wrapped in the night of four thousand years of barbarism, squatted there the 'equal' of their master, grinning at his forms of Justice, the evolution of forty centuries of Aryan genius. To their brute strength the white fanatic in the madness of his hate had appealed, and for their hire he had bartered the birthright of a mighty race of freemen." As Dixon's book gained wide popularity, the status of the Negro in popular literature reached its own nadir.

It was at this time and in this intellectual milieu that Wister published *The Virginian.* Scholars may argue the technical priority of other books as the "original" Western—Andy Adams, *The Log of a Cowboy* (1903), or B. M. Bower, *Chip of the Flying U* (1906)—but Wister's novel was the great archetype that established the Western as a distinct genre of popular fiction. Certainly it contained all the essential elements: a strong, simple and thoroughly good hero; a villain who was incarnate evil; a heroine who was pure and beautiful as well as stupid or stubborn enough to misunderstand or distrust the hero for at least half the story; large quantities of physical violence; and a final and fatal confrontation of good and evil. Certainly, too, it was enormously successful, going through fifteen printings during the first eight months after its publication; by 1911 it was in its thirty-eighth printing. By 1938 it had sold more than one and one-half million copies.

Wister's book was unlike most other great best-sellers in that it set the pattern for thousands of short stories, novels, motion pictures and television programs. Zane Grey, a New York dentist, was quick to recognize the possibilities of the pattern. He started with such "frontier" novels as *Betty Zane* (1903), but beginning with *Riders of the Purple Sage* (1912) he wrote more than fifty Western novels before his death. In the 1920s there was a great multiplication of Western novels and Western pulp magazines. So phenomenal was their success that they became, at least for a time, America's best-known contribution to popular literature.

The product was successful, and so it seemed foolish to vary the formula. An important part of that formula, just as it had been for Wister, was the Saxon pluck of the hero. Thus when Professor Walter Prescott Webb asked several magazine editors to give their reasons for the popularity of the Western story, here was one answer: "The Western story is the most popular type of action story. In order to give reasons for this, one thing must be recognized immediately: it is understood by us, and should be understood by everyone, that we are dealing with the popularity of Western stories as concerns the readers who are white, who may be called Nordics, using this term advisedly. The white race has always been noted for being hard-drinking, hard-fighting, fearless, fair and square." Quite obviously, the Negro cowboy, in fiction, was confronted with a color line over which he could not ride.

Today that color line cannot be drawn in quite the same way. Since World War II the Negro cowboy has been as infrequently in fiction as he was before the war, but his absence is accounted for in a different way. Most editors and writers have turned away from the kind of thoughtless racism openly expressed during the earlier part of the century. It can no longer be said that the continued maintenance of the color line in Western fiction is an expression of overt and conscious race prejudices.

Neither is it merely a matter of literary inertia, of unthinking repetition of formula. While it is true that popular commercial fiction clings desperately to stereotypes and is restrained by editorial taboos, many of the stereotypes have been shattered and many of the taboos abandoned in recent years. There has even been much talk of "adult" Westerns, in which the heroes have had some impure motives and the villains have been "good guys with emotional problems." Since World War II a bit of this growing up has become evident in some of the Western novels and stories of Ernest Haycox, Clay Fisher and Jack Schaefer.

Perhaps one sign of this new maturity has been the appearance of a few Negroes in stories about the West. One such story is "Stampede!" by Allan R. Bosworth, which appeared in *The Saturday Evening Post* in 1950. The story covers a drive up the Western Trail into Kansas, and Dan Robie, the Negro cowboy, is treated pretty much as the real Negro cowboy was treated on the actual drives up the Western Trail in the 1870s and 1880s.

On occasion, too, novelists have respected Western history. Walter Van Tilburg Clark in *The Ox-Bow Incident* (1940), set in Nevada in 1885, included in his large cast a Negro who had only a minor role physically but played a major part symbolically as the conscience of the others. *The Aristocrat*, by Genevieve Greer, developed an important secondary character in Abe, the old Negro who wore high heeled boots and a ten-gallon hat and still walked like the cowboy he had once been. In *The Wonderful Country* (1952), set in the Southwest after the Civil War, Tom Lea used Negro troops and a Negro sergeant who had once been a cowboy. But these novels are not "Westerns."

One possible explanation of the nearly complete white monopoly of roles in Western fiction and drama is the unique status of the cowboy as an American folk hero. Unlike other folk heroes, he is a kind of nameless Everyman, a symbol of the real or desired courage, independence and triumph of the ordinary American. As Lewis Atherton said, "virtually any schoolboy can name Daniel Boone as the symbol of the wilderness Indian fighter, Mike Fink and Davy Crockett as kings of the wild frontier, and Paul Bunyan as hero of the lumber camps. All of these characters, except possibly Boone, have been raised to the stature of Beowulfs of old—folk heroes, yes, but credited with feats that put them above the emulation of mortal man. But who is *the* great American cowboy? In answer, one must recognize that he continues to be a composite of many men, a nameless hero in recognition of the fact that his deeds were not beyond the powers of virtually anyone willing to exert his energies. His feats were great but not miraculous, and Americans have been reluctant to endow him with a superhuman personality. As a hero of the American folk, he is truly all of them in one." Such a hero, it was believed, could not be too clearly differentiated from most other Americans. He could not be a Swede, a German or an Englishman—though all of these were real cowboys—and he could not be a devout Mormon, Catholic or Jew. Like an "ideal" Presidential candidate, he was expected to be a white, Protestant American with whom most Americans can identify.

Yet even this explanation has now become unsatisfactory. Certainly recent history has shown a continuous decline in American bigotry. No particular religion is now necessarily a fatal handicap to a candidate for high office, and most of us have cheered for sports heroes of different races and religions. Americans are learning that one of their strengths—one of their glories—is unity in diversity. And in most popular fiction and drama, as well as in sports, show business and public life, that diversity is being represented.

Today, perhaps, ignorance of history is the most important reason that the Negro cowboy does not ride in fiction. Americans have assumed that because Negroes have not been in Western fiction they were never in the West. The prairie was different from the city, said one writer, for there the Jew, Negro and Italian never came. This attitude Americans accept as history, and what they learn is strangely incomplete.

The modern world learns about itself through its fiction, somewhat inaccurately. From reading Faulkner, Hemingway, Dos Passos, Steinbeck and Caldwell, the Frenchman sees the American man becoming immature, being obsessed with fears and having a "mixture of puritan-inspired neuroses and essential loneliness." When the 1957 riots in Little Rock made headlines all over the world, the sales of Harriet Beecher Stowe's *Uncle Tom's Cabin* rose in Helsinki. It is difficult to see how the Finns in reading a novel published in 1852 can have gained much insight into an American problem of 1957.

Writers and casting directors who have studied the old West and who know something of its diversity believe that they must respect the ignorance of their audience. They fear the incredulity of readers and viewers. They know that truth may be stranger than fiction, and hence less credible. They fear that the accurate representation of the Negro's role in the opening of the West would paradoxically seem to be a falsification of history.

Their fear may well be justified. Yet ignorance hurts everyone by impoverishing and cheapening a proud memory. Americans have lost something valuable if they forget that Wild Bill Hickok and George Washington Carver grew up on the Western plains at the same time. Americans need to remember that the West once nearly approached the democracy that they are still striving to achieve: "when a cowman sets out to hire help, he's not much concerned with a man's sex appeal or photogenic qualities; what he's looking for is a man who can get the job done, a *working* cowhand." In Philip Ashton Rollins's words, "The men who made the spirit of the West, who forbade Mason and Dixon's line to extend, who harnessed democracy, wore 'chaps.'" Americans need to remember that the Wyoming pioneers desegregated their first school; then maybe American history and fiction can one day be desegregated.

Perhaps all Americans may someday share in the heritage of the West. They may someday correct the injustice described by Dr. Frank P. Graham, former president of the University of North Carolina, when he wrote, "Negro children in school, in the library, at the moving picture, and over the radio, see and hear, and learn about white people. The picture in the school primer is always a picture of the white child." Eventually those Negro children may also see, hear and learn about some of their own great-grandfathers who broke wild horses, fought wilder Indians and rode in the choking dust behind great herds of cattle.

FOR DISCUSSION

1. A significant fact about American Western fiction is that most of the popular authors of this genre (from Erastus Beadle and Ned Buntline to Owen Wister) were native Easterners. What are some of the reasons for this Eastern fascination with the Western frontier? What was there about Eastern society (urban, industrialized, "civilized") which accounts for the popularity of Western novels from the late 1860s into the twentieth century? Why did these Eastern novelists tend to disregard the elements of the real West?

2. Philip Durham and Everett Jones place much of the blame for the White, Anglo-Saxon image of the West on Owen Wister's novel, *The Virginian.* After reading this section, do you agree that Wister's novel created this prototype image of the Westerner? Were the popular dime novelists of the nineteenth century also responsible for portraying a "lily-White" West? Explain.

3. What do you suppose accounts for the continuing high interest in Westerns in popular fiction?

PART THREE

The West As Fiction—
The Motion Picture Myth

No medium has done more to promote and popularize Western frontier mythology than the movies. Western films have always been a staple of the motion picture (and, later, television) industry. The first movie to tell a story was a Western—Edwin S. Porter's *The Great Train Robbery,* produced in 1903. From the earliest silents until today the heroic figure of the cowboy has dominated American movie screens. In 1971 the indefatigable John Wayne was American films' number one box office attraction on the basis of starring in three Westerns.

The traditional movie Westerner is an extension of the pages of Buntline and Wister, only more vivid and memorable. Hollywood has presented this bigger-than-life figure in a variety of cinematic vehicles. Epic Western films like the silents, *The Covered Wagon* and *The Iron Horse,* through the Cinerama production of *How the West Was Won* have cast the cowboy as the heroic builder of the nation, a kind of spiritual superpatriot. Perhaps even more influential, particularly in the pretelevision decades of the 1920s, 1930s, and 1940s, have been the cowboy stars of countless unsophisticated "B" pictures. Hundreds of these films saturated American movie screens for over thirty years, and Tom Mix, Gene Autry, and Roy Rogers, and countless others, were the idols of millions of little boys. The hero's white hat, his fast draw, his super horse, and his Texas drawl ("Howdy paardner") became a part of the twentieth-century American tradition. Indeed, only recently, with the notable exception of the popular John Wayne image, has the Western film begun to shy away from the standard heroics of the genre (see Part IV).

Many Western films have used historical themes as background for the heroic deeds of their stars. Almost always, "real" characters of the Old West have been considerably whitewashed for movie audiences. Wyatt Earp, Billy the Kid, Jesse James, George Armstrong Custer, Calamity Jane, and others have had their heroic screen counterparts time and time again. In their exhaustive study of the Western film, *The Western: From Silents to Cinerama,* cinema historians George Fenin and William K. Everson have pointed out the convenient way Hollywood has distorted the biographies of these figures of the Western past, as the excerpt from their book reprinted in this section indicates.

from The Western: From Silents to Cinerama

George N. Fenin and William K. Everson

The impact of [the Westward Movement] on successive decades of American life and progress has amply proved the frontier's existence in the hearts and minds of Americans as something much more appealing than a splendid historical period. The frontier is, in fact, the only mythological tissue available to this young nation. Gods and demigods, passions and ideals, the fatality of events, the sadness and glory of death, the struggle of good and evil—all these themes of the Western myth constitute an ideal ground for a liaison and re-elaboration of the Olympian world, a refreshing symbiotic relationship of Hellenic thought and Yankee dynamism.

The cowboy on horseback shapes into the fabulous Centaurus, guardian of a newly acquired legend; the woman—whose presence is biologically sought in the frontier town—becomes a sort of Minerva, dispensing wisdom, often moral principles, warm comfort, and unrelenting excitement and incitement; Marshal Wyatt Earp's exploits come strikingly close to the labors of Hercules, while William Frederick Cody's (Buffalo Bill) and Wild Bill Hickok's struggles with Indians and "badmen" are often recognized as the modern versions of the classic heroes. The massacre of the Seventh Cavalry at Little Big Horn carries the seed of fatality bearing down upon Oedipus, and the "Remember the Alamo!" reminds us of Thermopylae.

Above this epic looms the pathos of the fight between good and evil so dear to Anglo-Saxon hearts, a theme that finds its highest literary expression in Herman Melville's *Moby Dick*. An epoch such as this, representing the joint effort of a great heterogeneous people, sparked with the manifestations of a striking individualism, appealed to both the individualist and the collectivist. The conquest of nature and the law of the gun must have appealed to the first; the collectivist had his work cut out for him in the tremendous amount of organized effort needed to plow the earth, raise cattle, mine, create towns, counties, and cities. A state of mind evolved and it was accepted with enthusiasm in the eastern states. The literature it spawned must indicate this: from the *Western Journal* by Irving, followed by *Astoria, The Adventures of Captain Bonneville, U. S. A.* and *Tour of Prairies* to *Roughing It* by Twain, *The Luck of Roaring Camp* and *The Outcasts of Poker Flat* by Harte, *The Virginian* by Wister, and *Heart of the West* by O. Henry, *The Westerners* by White, *The Big Sky* by Guthrie, *Wyatt Earp* by Lake, *The Oregon Trail* by Parkman, *Crazy Horse* by Sandoz, *The Ox-Bow Incident* by Clark, and many others.

In the course of years, such literature increased continuously, and the names of authors like Ernest Haycox, Luke Short, Max Brand, Will Ermine,

Charles W. Webber, Emerson Hough, E. C. Mann and Zane Grey characterize a specific Western narrative in the form of novels, short stories, and essays which did not exert a substantial influence on the entire American culture, but which, nevertheless, gave body and form to a legend. We should also mention Clarence E. Mulford and William Colt MacDonald, above-average writers of standard Western novels, and writers much drawn upon by the movies. Mulford was first used by Tom Mix in the twenties, became more familiar later when his novels were filmed in the Hopalong Cassidy series. W. C. MacDonald's *3 Mesquiteer* Western novels inspired a few one-shot Western films, such as *Powdersmoke Range* (1935) and *Law of the 45's* (1935-6) and later a whole series at Republic Studios from 1937 to 1945. The term *mesquiteer* was obviously derived from the French *mousquetaire;* and *mesquite* is a form of prairie shrubbery.

The American legend was subsequently transformed, from the craftsman-like effort of the previous writers, into the smoothly organized, slickly presented assembly line product flooding America even today with books by the hundred, magazine stories and novelettes by the thousand. They have become an almost unbearable weight on the intellectual faced in most cases with tons of pulp publications of no value whatsoever. They cannot in any way aid in exactly evaluating the American western epic but the sociologist finds, in the specialized western essays and short stories, an effective ground for the study of their influence on the American public and its mores.

Hollywood and the Western novel

American western literature would have remained confined to the limited domains of folklore and a narrow literary genre or, at best, to the specialized field of history if the birth of motion pictures had not exerted the stupendous verdict of their own possibilities. . . .

At the beginning of the twentieth century, the United States was still a land of opportunity where private enterprise bordered often on unscrupulous and illegal practices, and adventure appealed to hardy individuals. The California Gold Rush and the Great Cattle Depression of 1886-87, among many events, made outlaws and gunfighters of many cowboys; though they were already part of a colorful past, banditry had not disappeared.

On August 29, 1900, a few minutes after 8 P.M., train no. 3 of the Union Pacific Railroad Company, after having passed the station at Tipton, Wyoming, began to slow down as it approached Table Rock. Four men emerged from the darkness, forced the conductor, E. J. Kerrigan, to uncouple the passenger cars while the express and mail cars were pulled a mile distant and subsequently robbed. The thieves were some of the Wild Bunch boys: Butch Cassidy, Deaf Charlie Hanks, Bill Carver, Harvey Logan. The raid netted a little more than five thousand dollars in cash and a few hundred dollars' worth of watch movements, and reconfirmed their fame as "the largest, toughest and most colorful of all Western outlaw gangs. . . . The first such aggregation to have an orderly organization," as stated by James P. Horan and Paul Sann in their *Pictorial History of the Wild West*. In a special article that appeared three years later, when the Pinkerton detectives had already killed or arrested the majority of the gang's members, the *Denver Daily News* revealed that the Wild Bunch outlaws had caused Governor Wells of Utah to contact the governors of Colorado and Wyoming in order to create a concerted plan of action to combat the menace.

Such exploits vividly aroused popular fantasy, and the traditional sympathy of the American masses for the underdog, fanned by sensational newspaper reports, provided ideal ground for the emergence of the myth of the outlaw. They provided ground, too, for the physical expression of those stark puritanical values implicit in the struggle between good and evil, which have so affected the American unconscious as revealed in the country's folkways and mores. Even if the Koster and Bial Music Hall's first showing of "moving pictures" on April 23, 1896, brought to the American public visions of sea waves breaking upon the shores, as well as some comic vaudeville items, and even if factual events continued to attract attention, the growing demand for theatrical films became hard to dent. This phenomenon, stimulated as well by the urge to contemplate something more realistic and dramatic, materialized ultimately and, after many attempts at cinematic storytelling, in 1903 Edwin S. Porter made his *The Great Train Robbery*. Lewis Jacobs in his *The Rise of the American Film* said the film "has since represented the Bible of the film-makers." Actually this somewhat exaggerates its personal value, but until 1909 it did have a very great deal of influence.

From then on, the Western was a genre of the American cinema. It also was the vehicle through which motion pictures and the public consorted in a remarkable symbiotic relationship. The fact that the motion picture, this "flower and crown of the twentieth century," could express in indisputably effective terms the magnitude of the recent American saga, an essential force still permeating the lives and the philosophy of life of great masses of the people, was accepted with enthusiasm by a public anxious to learn quickly of its pioneer heritage, in order to acquire fundamental principles for its destiny.

Thus, from that year which represented the birth of film Westerns, that year which saw the headlines of the nation's dailies echo the most recent exploit of the Wild Bunch, the film-makers began a long and exciting march, the milestones of which were represented—after an adolescence—by an epic school, the sound era, color, wide screen . . . right up to the present film, a Western very different from the one imagined by Edwin S. Porter. The Western of today seems to be choosing some rather offbeat paths, and the psychological, sophisticated, "adult tale" of the West is proof of this evolution. In these more than fifty years we have seen one of the most amazing cases of a deliberate manipulation of a nation's history in the hands of a powerful group of film-makers.

The drab and grim frontier, with its people struggling for existence as ranchers, farmers and merchants was depicted to movie audiences in an often entirely different fashion. All of the West's mushrooming communities—many of them peaceful and monotonous, heroic only in their dedication to the building of a new empire—became compressed into a stock formula town, the prototypes of Tombstone and Dodge City, with rustlers, desperadoes, and outlaws roaming the streets, or engaged in bloody saloon fights.

The great cattle empire, the gold and silver rushes, and the covered wagon treks were some of the phases of the West's history which the movies implied were a "permanent" part of the Western scene; actually, these phases were all of fairly short duration. Life in the old West was certainly a lawless one in many communities, but the generalized concept of the shooting down of endless villains and ranchers without so much as a second glance at the corpses is very much at odds with fact. A killing was as serious a matter in the West as it was in the East, although admittedly the justice meted out was a less standardized one. The laws of mob and vigilante groups were not inclined to temper justice with mercy and understanding, and in territories where the forces of crime and corruption outweighed those of law and order, an open and acknowledged felony might go unpunished. But regardless of the varying degrees of justice, even taking into account a "kill-or-be-killed" attitude among men who made their living outside the law, the taking of a human life was still not regarded lightly. The Westerns of William S. Hart recognized this principle; there was no casual extermination of badmen in the Hart-Ince pictures and among recent Westerns, Lesley Selander's *Stampede* (1949) was one of very few films which treated killing seriously.

In the glamorization of the outlaw, Hollywood has contradicted itself on many occasions, in addition to contradicting history. In *Badmen's Territory* (1946) the outlaw Sam Bass is played as a villain, in completely evil fashion by fat, swarthy Nestor Paiva. When Universal-International later made *Calamity Jane and Sam Bass* (1949)—inventing a fictional romance between the two—Bass was portrayed as the misunderstood hero played by clean-cut Howard Duff.

Reconstruction of historical events was and still is changed to suit the script; sympathetic or unsympathetic portrayals of events are often dependent on the importance of an historical character in a specific script. In *They Died With Their Boots On* (1941), Errol Flynn plays General Custer, depicted as a brilliant soldier, sympathetic to the Indians, whose command was ruthlessly massacred in a battle brought on by political chicanery. In *Sitting Bull* (1954) the story was told primarily from the Indian viewpoint: Sitting Bull was literally forced into battle by the stupidity and double-dealing of Custer, played in bullheaded fashion by Douglas Kennedy. Custer was an Indian-hater opposed to the efforts of hero Dale Robertson to effect a peace treaty. Another Indian-oriented work, *Chief Crazy Horse* (1955), gave that sachem, instead, the credit for the Little Big Horn battle, putting Sitting Bull in the position of a casual supervisor. The Warner film, *Santa Fe Trail* (1940) showed Custer, a lesser character in the film, graduating from West Point in the accustomed manner. Yet in *They Died With Their Boots On*, in which Custer was the main figure, a film made by the same studio only a year later, the audience saw General Sheridan commissioning Custer before his graduation and dispatching him forthwith to Washington where Union forces, expecting a Confederate attack momentarily, were desperately short of manpower. Here we have a clear-cut example of historical incident being manipulated to suit script requirements.

Historical events apart, neither film presented a very realistic picture of Custer the man. In *Santa Fe Trail,* played by Ronald Reagan, he was a quiet, sincere, and dedicated soldier; as written for Errol Flynn, he became the embodiment of the daredevil soldier, contemptuous of orders, more concerned with a fight for its own sake than for its underlying causes. Later, of course, according to this particular script, he became something of an idealist. In actuality, brilliant soldier or not, Custer had a mass of neurotic complexes—an aspect of him that no motion picture has yet presented, although there were good hints of it in the distinctly and deliberately critical and unpleasant Custer portrait presented in *Sitting Bull.*

One wonders now whether or not movie traditions sometimes have a more lasting effect than the authentic traditions they copy. For example, Custer's famed Seventh Cavalry, wiped out at the Little Big Horn, was subsequently reformed as a cavalry unit and retained as a permanent force in the United States Army. The Seventh Cavalry is still in action today and, like Custer himself, it utilizes flamboyant accessories to glamorize a regulation uniform—including cavalry boots, a western-style neckerchief and, among the officers, cavalry sabres. From several first-hand accounts, it seems that these "descendants" of Custer adopt a swaggering behavior more than casually related to, although somewhat enlarged upon, the behavior of the cavalry officers in a John Ford super-Western.

Hollywood's portrayal of Geronimo created the false impression that the Apaches were the most warlike Indians of all. Actually, although savage fighters, they were comparatively few in number, and far less troublesome than many lesser-known tribes. The capture of Geronimo, too, has been fictionalized in diverse ways, especially in the film *Geronimo* (1939), in which he is captured attempting to kill a white trader in a cavalry encampment. Another Western, *I Killed Geronimo* (1950), had him killed off in a last-reel fist fight. Universal's *Walk the Proud Land* (1956) finally told the true and comparatively straight-forward account of how the warrior was induced to surrender. The serious approach of William S. Hart, the singular—although romanticized—interpretation of John Ford, the wholly or partially rigorous renditions of David W. Griffith, Thomas Ince, James Cruze and other film-makers concerning the true atmosphere of the old West are drowned in a sea of distorted, standardized clichés. The American public, in part at least, recognized these clichés for the counter-feits they were. It is this same public, largely the Eastern audience, which has lately indicated its approval and acceptance of a more realistic and historically accurate treatment.

A new cycle has thus emerged in the contemporary cinema. In the past, Hollywood frequently used the Western as a proving ground for directors many of whom later achieved fame in other genres (e.g. Edward Dmytryk, William Wyler) and planned its Western output almost on the basis of calculated laboratory formula. Now, without new inspiration, Hollywood found itself regarding its perennial bread-and-butter in a new light. The renewed success and popularity of the Western, stimulated by the dumping of literally hundreds of "B" Westerns on television, has led to a gradual revamping of policies, toward a recognition of the need to present the West in more realistic terms. This has taken place in the midst of a competitive situation in which Hollywood has had to produce fewer films, of better quality.

The ultra-streamlined Westerns of Autry and Rogers brought together, in weird fashion, the standard ingredients of the old-time Westerns (chases, cattle stampedes, gunslinging, saloon fights) with contemporary elements (night clubs, radio, television, chorus girls, high-powered cars, jet-rockets, uranium deposits). Although Autry and Rogers no longer make theatrical Westerns, they often incorporate these innovations—admittedly to a much lesser degree than hitherto—into their television Westerns. And, of course, their late theatrical Westerns do still occasionally play in American theatres and more frequently on television. They are still regularly seen in Europe, always slower to absorb the huge quantities of "B" Westerns. Thus, old and new Westerns are available side by side, to further cloud the already confusing issues.

Today, the main street of Dodge City is a drab and rather unattractive artery, without the slightest resemblance to the picturesque terminal of the western trail. Tombstone jealously preserves its Crystal Palace Saloon, the old headquarters of Wyatt Earp's enemies. Deadwood survives as a little city in South Dakota, earning its money from the gold industry and the exhibition of an assortment of fake Wild Bill Hickok relics, including Wild Bill's "death chair," complete with bullet holes and painted bloodstains. A series of towns tries to perpetuate the tradition of the old West to attract tourist business; Covered Wagon Day, Pioneer's Day, Frontier Days, Old Times are some of the celebrations periodically organized, with a shrewd commercial instinct, in cities and towns like Prescott, Fort Worth, Cheyenne, Dodge City, and Gallup. The last laugh in the adulteration of the Wild West is represented by Las Vegas, a small Mormon center founded in 1855, and maintained by that religious body for more than fifty years as a devout community refusing to consider itself a part of the generally lawless era in which it lived. Today gambling and easy divorce bring masses of Americans to the modern part of the city, and while the old section continues its calm and uneventful existence, the fabulous gambling halls of the new city (where floor shows can afford to pay a well-shaped chorus girl two hundred dollars a week plus, and hire famous show-business entertainers) aim for an ever larger business running into millions of dollars. The Las Vegas "cowboys" today are not the grim and unshaven gunfighters of old, but "plain folk" from all parts of the Union, dressed in gaudy outfits. The Las Vegas cowboys are the products created by Hollywood, and the grotesque masquerade in only one way connects up with the open towns of another time: if Las Vegas is more or less open today, it is because the underworld has really gone underground in respectable clothing.

Ten Commandments of the Cowboy

[The countless "B" Westerns of the pretelevision era had great impact on American youth. The code of the Westerner served as a moral influence on society. Reprinted here is Gene Autry's famous "Ten Commandments of the Cowboy," written at the height of this actor's popularity in the late 1930s and praised by the film industry, boys' clubs, parents' groups, and churches.]

1. A cowboy never takes unfair advantage—even of an enemy.

2. A cowboy never betrays a trust.

3. A cowboy always tells the truth.

4. A cowboy is kind to small children, to old folks, and to animals.

5. A cowboy is free from racial and religious prejudice.

6. A cowboy is helpful and when anyone's in trouble he lends a hand.

7. A cowboy is a good worker.

8. A cowboy is clean about his person and in thought, word, and deed.

9. A cowboy respects womanhood, his parents, and the laws of his country.

10. A cowboy is a patriot.

Gene Autry. Courtesy of United Artists 16.

Movie Chronicle: The Westerner

Robert Warshow

[Probably the most famous serious analysis of the Western film ever written is Robert Warshow's essay, "The Westerner." In it Warshow examines the moral code of the Western by analyzing some of the better-known films of the 1930s, 1940s, and 1950s (*The Virginian, My Darling Clementine, The Gunfighter, High Noon,* and *Shane*). Through this analysis he attempts to explain the Western film as a distinct extension of American culture.]

They that have power to hurt and will do none,
That do not do the thing they most do show,
Who, moving others, are themselves as stone,
Unmoved, cold, and to temptation slow;
They rightly do inherit heaven's graces,
And husband nature's riches from expense;
They are the lords and owners of their faces,
Others but stewards of their excellence.[1]

The two most successful creations of American movies are the gangster and the Westerner: men with guns. Guns as physical objects, and the postures associated with their use, form the visual and emotional center of both types of films. I suppose this reflects the importance of guns in the fantasy life of Americans; but that is a less illuminating point than it appears to be.

The gangster movie, which no longer exists in its "classical" form, is a story of enterprise and success ending in precipitate failure. Success is conceived as an increasing power to work injury, it belongs to the city, and it is of course a form of evil (though the gangster's death, presented usually as "punishment," is perceived simply as defeat). The peculiarity of the gangster is his unceasing, nervous activity. The exact nature of his enterprises may remain vague, but his commitment to enterprise is always clear, and all the more clear because he operates outside the field of utility. He is without culture, without manners, without leisure, or at any rate his leisure is likely to be spent in debauchery so compulsively aggressive as to seem only another aspect of his "work." But he is graceful, moving like a dancer among the crowded dangers of the city.

Like other tycoons, the gangster is crude in conceiving his ends but by no means inarticulate; on the contrary, he is usually expansive and noisy (the introspective gangster is a fairly recent development), and can state definitely

---

1. William Shakespeare, Sonnet 94.

From **The Immediate Experience** by Robert Warshow, published by Doubleday & Company, Inc. Reprinted by permission of Paul Warshow.

what he wants: to take over the North Side, to own a hundred suits, to be Number One. But new "frontiers" will present themselves infinitely, and by a rigid convention it is understood that as soon as he wishes to rest on his gains, he is on the way to destruction.

The gangster is lonely and melancholy, and can give the impression of a profound worldly wisdom. He appeals most to adolescents with their impatience and their feeling of being outsiders, but more generally he appeals to that side of all of us which refuses to believe in the "normal" possibilities of happiness and achievement; the gangster is the "no" to that great American "yes" which is stamped so big over our official culture and yet has so little to do with the way we really feel about our lives. But the gangster's loneliness and melancholy are not "authentic"; like everything else that belongs to him, they are not honestly come by: he is lonely and melancholy not because life ultimately demands such feelings but because he has put himself in a position where everybody wants to kill him and eventually somebody will. He is wide open and defenseless, incomplete because unable to accept any limits or come to terms with his own nature, fearful, loveless. And the story of his career is a nightmare inversion of the values of ambition and opportunity. From the window of Scarface's bullet-proof apartment can be seen an electric sign proclaiming: "The World Is Yours," and, if I remember, this sign is the last thing we see after Scarface lies dead in the street. In the end it is the gangster's weakness as much as his power and freedom that appeals to us; the world is not ours, but it is not his either, and in his death he "pays" for our fantasies, releasing us momentarily both from the concept of success, which he denies by caricaturing it, and from the need to succeed, which he shows to be dangerous.

The Western hero, by contrast, is a figure of repose. He resembles the gangster in being lonely and to some degree melancholy. But his melancholy comes from the "simple" recognition that life is unavoidably serious, not from the disproportions of his own temperament. And his loneliness is organic, not imposed on him by his situation but belonging to him intimately and testifying to his completeness. The gangster must reject others violently or draw them violently to him. The Westerner is not thus compelled to seek love; he is prepared to accept it, perhaps, but he never asks of it more than it can give, and we see him constantly in situations where love is at best an irrelevance. If there is a woman he loves, she is usually unable to understand his motives; she is against killing and being killed, and he finds it impossible to explain to her that there is no point in being "against" these things: they belong to his world.

Very often this woman is from the East and her failure to understand represents a clash of cultures. In the American mind, refinement, virtue, civilization, Christianity itself, are seen as feminine, and therefore women are often portrayed as possessing some kind of deeper wisdom, while the men, for all their apparent self-assurance, are fundamentally childish. But the West, lacking the graces of civilization, is the place "where men are men"; in Western movies, men have the deeper wisdom and the women are children. Those women in the

Western movies who share the hero's understanding of life are prostitutes (or, as they are usually presented, barroom entertainers)—women, that is, who have come to understand in the most practical way how love can be an irrelevance, and therefore "fallen" women. The gangster, too, associates with prostitutes, but for him the important things about a prostitute are her passive availability and her costliness: she is part of his winnings. In Western movies, the important thing about a prostitute is her quasi-masculine independence: nobody owns her, nothing has to be explained to her, and she is not, like a virtuous woman, a "value" that demands to be protected. When the Westerner leaves the prostitute for a virtuous woman—for love—he is in fact forsaking a way of life, though the point of the choice is often obscured by having the prostitute killed by getting into the line of fire.

The Westerner is *par excellence* a man of leisure. Even when he wears the badge of a marshal or, more rarely, owns a ranch, he appears to be unemployed. We see him standing at a bar, or playing poker—a game which expresses perfectly his talent for remaining relaxed in the midst of tension—or perhaps camping out on the plains on some extraordinary errand. If he does own a ranch, it is in the background; we are not actually aware that he owns anything except his horse, his guns, and the one worn suit of clothing which is likely to remain unchanged all through the movie. It comes as a surprise to see him take money from his pocket or an extra shirt from his saddlebags. As a rule we do not even know where he sleeps at night and don't think of asking. Yet it never occurs to us that he is a poor man; there is no poverty in Western movies, and really no wealth either: those great cattle domains and shipments of gold which figure so largely in the plots are moral and not material quantities, not the objects of contention but only its occasion. Possessions too are irrelevant.

Employment of some kind—usually unproductive—is always open to the Westerner, but when he accepts it, it is not because he needs to make a living, much less from any idea of "getting ahead." Where could he want to "get ahead" to? By the time we see him, he is already "there": he can ride a horse faultlessly, keep his countenance in the face of death, and draw his gun a little faster and shoot it a little straighter than anyone he is likely to meet. These are sharply defined acquirements, giving to the figure of the Westerner an apparent moral clarity which corresponds to the clarity of his physical image against his bare landscape; initially, at any rate, the Western movie presents itself as being without mystery, its whole universe comprehended in what we see on the screen.

Much of this apparent simplicity arises directly from those "cinematic" elements which have long been understood to give the Western theme its special appropriateness for the movies: the wide expanses of land, the free movement of men on horses. As guns constitute the visible moral center of the Western movie, suggesting continually the possibility of violence, so land and horses represent the movie's material basis, its sphere of action. But the land and the horses have also a moral significance: the physical freedom they represent belongs to the moral "openness" of the West—corresponding to the fact that guns are carried where they can be seen. (And, as we shall see, the character of land and horses changes as the Western film becomes more complex.)

The gangster's world is less open, and his arts not so easily identifiable as the Westerner's. Perhaps he too can keep his countenance, but the mask he wears is really no mask: its purpose is precisely to make evident the fact that he desperately wants to "get ahead" and will stop at nothing. Where the Westerner imposes himself by the appearance of unshakable control, the gangster's pre-eminence lies in the suggestion that he may at any moment lose control; his strength is not in being able to shoot faster or straighter than others, but in being more willing to shoot. "Do it first," says Scarface expounding his mode of operation, "and keep on doing it!" With the Westerner, it is a crucial point of honor *not* to "do it first"; his gun remains in its holster until the moment of combat.

There is no suggestion, however, that he draws the gun reluctantly. The Westerner could not fulfill himself if the moment did not finally come when he can shoot his enemy down. But because that moment is so thoroughly the expression of his being, it must be kept pure. He will not violate the accepted forms of combat though by doing so he could save a city. And he can wait. "When you call me that—smile!"—the villain smiles weakly, soon he is laughing with horrible joviality, and the crisis is past. But it is allowed to pass because it must come again: sooner or later Trampas will "make his play," and the Virginian will be ready for him.

What does the Westerner fight for? We know he is on the side of justice and order, and of course it can be said he fights for these things. But such broad aims never correspond exactly to his real motives; they only offer him his opportunity. The Westerner himself, when an explanation is asked of him (usually by a woman), is likely to say that he does what he "has to do." If justice and order did not continually demand his protection, he would be without a calling. Indeed, we come upon him often in just that situation, as the reign of law settles over the West and he is forced to see that his day is over; those are the pictures which end with his death or with his departure for some more remote frontier. What he defends, at bottom, is the purity of his own image—in fact his honor. This is what makes him invulnerable. When the gangster is killed, his whole life is shown to have been a mistake, but the image the Westerner seeks to maintain can be presented as clearly in defeat as in victory: he fights not for advantage and not for the right, but to state what he is, and he must live in a world which permits that statement. The Westerner is the last gentleman, and the movies which over and over again tell his story are probably the last art form in which the concept of honor retains its strength.

Of course I do not mean to say that ideas of virtue and justice and courage have gone out of culture. Honor is more than these things: it is a style, concerned with harmonious appearances as much as with desirable conse-quences, and tending therefore toward the denial of life in favor of art. "Who hath it? he that died o' Wednesday." On the whole, a world that leans to

Falstaff's view is a more civilized and even, finally, a more graceful world. It is just the march of civilization that forces the Westerner to move on; and if we actually had to confront the question it might turn out that the woman who refuses to understand him is right as often as she is wrong. But we do not confront the question. Where the Westerner lives it is always about 1870—not the real 1870, either, or the real West—and he is killed or goes away when his position becomes problematical. The fact that he continues to hold our attention is evidence enough that, in his proper frame, he presents an image of personal nobility that is still real for us.

Clearly, this image easily becomes ridiculous: we need only look at William S. Hart or Tom Mix, who in the wooden absoluteness of their virtue represented little that an adult could take seriously; and doubtless such figures as Gene Autry or Roy Rogers are no better, though I confess I have seen none of their movies. Some film enthusiasts claim to find in the early, unsophisticated Westerns a "cinematic purity" that has since been lost. . . . The truth is that the Westerner comes into the field of serious art only when his moral code, without ceasing to be compelling, is seen also to be imperfect. The Westerner at his best exhibits a moral ambiguity which darkens his image and saves him from absurdity; this ambiguity arises from the fact that, whatever his justifications, he is a killer of men.

In *The Virginian,* which is an archetypal Western movie as *Scarface* or *Little Caesar* are archetypal gangster movies, there is a lynching in which the hero (Gary Cooper), as leader of a posse, must supervise the hanging of his best friend for stealing cattle. With the growth of American "social consciousness," it is no longer possible to present a lynching in the movies unless the point is the illegality and injustice of the lynching itself; *The Ox-Bow Incident,* made in 1943, explicitly puts forward the newer point of view and can be regarded as a kind of "anti-Western." But in 1929, when *The Virginian* was made, the present inhibition about lynching was not yet in force; the justice, and therefore the necessity, of the hanging is never questioned—except by the schoolteacher from the East, whose refusal to understand serves as usual to set forth more sharply the deeper seriousness of the West. The Virginian is thus in a tragic dilemma where one moral absolute conflicts with another and the choice of either must leave a moral stain. If he had chosen to save his friend, he would have violated the image of himself that he had made essential to his existence, and the movie would have had to end with his death, for only by his death could the image have been restored. Having chosen instead to sacrifice his friend to the higher demands of the "code"—the only choice worthy of him, as even the friend understands—he is none the less stained by the killing, but what is needed now to set accounts straight is not his death but the death of the villain Trampas, the leader of the cattle thieves, who had escaped the posse and abandoned the Virginian's friend to his fate. Again the woman intervenes: Why must there be *more* killing? If the hero really loved her, he would leave town, refusing Trampas's challenge. What good will it be if Trampas should kill him? But the

Virginian does once more what he "has to do," and in avenging his friend's death wipes out the stain on his own honor. Yet his victory cannot be complete: no death can be paid for and no stain truly wiped out; the movie is still a tragedy, for though the hero escapes with his life, he has been forced to confront the ultimate limits of his moral ideas.

This mature sense of limitation and unavoidable guilt is what gives the Westerner a "right" to his melancholy. It is true that the gangster's story is also a tragedy—in certain formal ways more clearly a tragedy than the Westerner's—but it is a romantic tragedy, based on a hero whose defeat springs with almost mechanical inevitability from the outrageous presumption of his demands: the gangster is *bound* to go on until he is killed. The Westerner is a more classical figure, self-contained and limited to begin with, seeking not to extend his dominion but only to assert his personal value, and his tragedy lies in the fact that even this circumscribed demand cannot be fully realized. Since the Westerner is not a murderer but (most of the time) a man of virtue, and since he is always prepared for defeat, he retains his inner invulnerability and his story need not end with his death (and usually does not); but what we finally respond to is not his victory but his defeat.

Up to a point, it is plain that the deeper seriousness of the good Western films comes from the introduction of a realism, both physical and psychological, that was missing with Tom Mix and William S. Hart. As lines of age have come into Gary Cooper's face since *The Virginian,* so the outlines of the Western movie in general have become less smooth, its background more drab. The sun still beats upon the town, but the camera is likely now to take advantage of this illumination to seek out more closely the shabbiness of buildings and furniture, the loose, worn hang of clothing, the wrinkles and dirt of the faces. Once it has been discovered that the true theme of the Western movie is not the freedom and expansiveness of frontier life, but its limitations, its material bareness, the pressures of obligation, then even the landscape itself ceases to be quite the arena of free movement it once was, but becomes instead a great empty waste, cutting down more often than it exaggerates the stature of the horseman who rides across it. We are more likely now to see the Westerner struggling against the obstacles of the physical world (as in the wonderful scenes on the desert and among the rocks in *The Last Posse*) than carelessly surmounting them. Even the horses, no longer the "friends" of man or the inspired chargers of knight-errantry, have lost much of the moral significance that once seemed to belong to them in their careering across the screen. It seems to me the horses grow tired and stumble more often than they did, and that we see them less frequently at the gallop.

In *The Gunfighter,* a remarkable film of a couple of years ago, the landscape has virtually disappeared. Most of the action takes place indoors, in a cheerless saloon where a tired "bad man" (Gregory Peck) contemplates the waste of his life, to be senselessly killed at the end by a vicious youngster setting off on the same futile path. The movie is done in cold, quiet tones of gray, and every object in it—faces, clothing, a table, the hero's heavy mustache—is given an air of uncompromising authenticity, suggesting those dim photographs of the nineteenth-century West in which Wyatt Earp, say, turns out to be a blank untidy figure posing awkwardly before some uninteresting building. This "authenticity," to be sure, is only aesthetic; the chief fact about nineteenth-century photographs, to my eyes at any rate, is how stonily they refuse to yield up the truth. But that limitation is just what is needed: by preserving some hint of the rigidity of archaic photography (only in tone and décor, never in composition), *The Gunfighter* can permit us to feel that we are looking at a more "real" West than the one the movies have accustomed us to—harder, duller, less "romantic"—and yet without forcing us outside the boundaries which give the Western movie its validity.

We come upon the hero of *The Gunfigher* at the end of a career in which he has never upheld justice and order, and has been at times, apparently, an actual criminal; in this case, it is clear that the hero has been wrong and the woman who has rejected his way of life has been right. He is thus without any of the larger justifications, and knows himself a ruined man. There can be no question of his "redeeming" himself in any socially constructive way. He is too much the victim of his own reputation to turn marshal as one of his old friends has done, and he is not offered the sentimental solution of a chance to give up his life for some good end; the whole point is that he exists outside the field of social value. Indeed, if we were once allowed to see him in the days of his "success," he might become a figure like the gangster, for his career has been aggressively "anti-social" and the practical problem he faces is the gangster's problem: there will always be somebody trying to kill him. Yet it is obviously absurd to speak of him as "anti-social," not only because we do not see him acting as a criminal, but more fundamentally because we do not see his milieu as a society. Of course it has its "social problems" and a kind of static history: civilization is always just at the point of driving out the old freedom; there are women and children to represent the possibility of a settled life; and there is the marshal, a bad man turned good, determined to keep at least his area of jurisdiction at peace. But these elements are not, in fact, a part of the film's "realism," even though they come out of the real history of the West; they belong to the conventions of the form, to that accepted framework which makes the film possible in the first place, and they exist not to provide a standard by which the gunfighter can be judged, but only to set him off. The true "civilization" of the Western movie is always embodied in an individual, good or bad is more a matter of personal bearing than of social consequences, and the conflict of good and bad is a duel between two men. Deeply troubled and obviously doomed, the gunfighter is the Western hero still, perhaps all the more because his value must express itself entirely in his own being—in his presence, the way he holds our eyes—and in contradiction to the facts. No matter what he has done, he *looks* right, and he remains invulnerable because, without acknowledging anyone else's right to judge him, he has judged his own failure and has already assimilated it, understanding—as no one else understands except the marshal and the barroom girl—that he can do nothing but play out the drama of the gun fight again and again until the time comes when it will be he who gets killed. What "redeems" him is that he no longer believes in this drama and nevertheless will continue to play his role perfectly: the pattern is all.

The proper function of realism in the Western movie can only be to deepen the lines of that pattern. It is an art form for connoisseurs, where the spectator derives his pleasure from the appreciation of minor variations within the working out of a pre-established order. One does not want too much novelty: it comes as a shock, for instance, when the hero is made to operate without a gun, as has been done in several pictures (e.g., *Destry Rides Again*), and our uneasiness is allayed only when he is finally compelled to put his "pacifism" aside. If the hero can be shown to be troubled, complex, fallible, even eccentric, or the villain given some psychological taint or, better, some evocative physical mannerism, to shade the colors of his villainy, that is all to the good. Indeed, that kind of variation is absolutely necessary to keep the type from becoming sterile; we do not want to see the same movie over and over again, only the same form. But when the impulse toward realism is extended into a "reinterpretation" of the West as a developed society, drawing our eyes away from the hero if only to the extent of showing him as the one dominant figure in a complex social order, then the pattern is broken and the West itself begins to be uninteresting. If the "social problems" of the frontier are to be the movie's chief concern, there is no longer any point in re-examining these problems twenty times a year; they have been solved, and the people for whom they once were real are dead. Moreover, the hero himself, still the film's central figure, now tends to become its one unassimilable element, since he is the most "unreal."

The Ox-Bow Incident, by denying the convention of the lynching, presents us with a modern "social drama" and evokes a corresponding response, but in doing so it almost makes the Western setting irrelevant, a mere backdrop of beautiful scenery. (It is significant that *The Ox-Bow Incident* has no hero; a hero would have to stop the lynching or be killed in trying to stop it, and then the "problem" of lynching would no longer be central.) Even in *The Gunfighter* the women and children are a little too much in evidence, threatening constantly to become a real focus of concern instead of simply part of the given framework; and the young tough who kills the hero has too much the air of juvenile criminality: the hero himself could never have been like that, and the idea of a cycle being repeated therefore loses its sharpness. But the most striking example of the confusion created by a too conscientious "social" realism is in the celebrated *High Noon*.

In *High Noon* we find Gary Cooper still the upholder of order that he was in *The Virginian,* but twenty-four years older, stooped, slower moving, awkward, his face lined, the flesh sagging, a less beautiful and weaker figure, but with the suggestion of greater depth that belongs almost automatically to age. Like the hero of *The Gunfighter,* he no longer has to assert his character and is no longer interested in the drama of combat; it is hard to imagine that he might once have been so youthful as to say, "When you call me that—smile!" In fact, when we come upon him he is hanging up his guns and his marshal's badge in order to begin a new, peaceful life with his bride, who is a Quaker. But then the news comes that a man he had sent to prison has been pardoned and will get to town on the noon train; three friends of this man have come to wait for him at the station, and when the freed convict arrives the four of them will come to kill the marshal. He is thus trapped; the bride will object, the hero himself will waver much more than he would have done twenty-four years ago, but in the end he will play out the drama because it is what he "has to do." All this belongs to the established form (there is even the "fallen woman" who understands the marshal's position as his wife does not). Leaving aside the crudity of building up suspense by means of the clock, the actual Western drama of *High Noon* is well handled and forms a good companion piece to *The Virginian,* showing in both conception and technique the ways in which the Western movie has naturally developed.

But there is a second drama along with the first. As the marshal sets out to find deputies to help him deal with the four gunmen, we are taken through the various social strata of the town, each group in turn refusing its assistance out of cowardice, malice, irresponsibility, or venality. With this we are in the field of "social drama"—of a very low order, incidentally, altogether unconvincing and displaying a vulgar anti-populism that has marred some other movies of Stanley Kramer's. But the falsity of the "social drama" is less important than the fact that it does not belong in the movie to begin with. The technical problem was to make it necessary for the marshal to face his enemies alone; to explain *why* the other townspeople are not at his side is to raise a question which does not exist in the proper frame of the Western movie, where the hero is "naturally" alone and it is only necessary to contrive the physical absence of those who might be his allies, if any contrivance is needed at all. In addition, though the hero of *High Noon* proves himself a better man than all around him, the actual effect of this contrast is to lessen his stature: he becomes only a rejected man of virtue. In our final glimpse of him, as he rides away through the town where he has spent most of his life without really imposing himself on it, he is a pathetic rather than a tragic figure. And his departure has another meaning as well; the "social drama" has no place for him.

But there is also a different way of violating the Western form. This is to yield entirely to its static quality as legend and to the "cinematic" temptations of its landscape, the horses, the quiet men. John Ford's famous *Stagecoach* (1938) had much of this unhappy preoccupation with style, and the same director's *My Darling Clementine* (1946), a soft and beautiful movie about Wyatt Earp, goes further along the same path, offering indeed a superficial accuracy of historical reconstruction, but so loving in execution as to destroy the outlines of the Western legend, assimilating it to the more sentimental legend of rural America and making the hero a more dangerous Mr. Deeds. (*Powder*

River, a recent "routine" Western shamelessly copied from *My Darling Clemen-tine,* is in most ways a better film; lacking the benefit of a serious director, it is necessarily more concerned with drama than with style.)

The highest expression of this aestheticizing tendency is in George Stevens' *Shane,* where the legend of the West is virtually reduced to its essentials and then fixed in the dreamy clarity of a fairy tale. There never was so broad and bare and lovely a landscape as Stevens puts before us, or so unimaginably comfortless a "town" as the little group of buildings on the prairie to which the settlers must come for their supplies and to buy a drink. The mere physical progress of the film, following the style of *A Place in the Sun,* is so deliberately graceful that everything seems to be happening at the bottom of a clear lake. The hero (Alan Ladd) is hardly a man at all, but something like the Spirit of the West, beautiful in fringed buckskins. He emerges mysteriously from the plains, breathing sweet-ness and a melancholy which is no longer simply the Westerner's natural response to experience but has taken on spirituality; and when he has accom-plished his mission, meeting and destroying in the black figure of Jack Palance a Spirit of Evil just as metaphysical as his own embodiment of virtue, he fades away again into the more distant West, a man whose "day is over," leaving behind the wondering little boy who might have imagined the whole story. The choice of Alan Ladd to play the leading role is alone an indication of this film's tendency. Actors like Gary Cooper or Gregory Peck are in themselves, as material objects, "realistic," seeming to bear in their bodies and their faces mortality, limitation, the knowledge of good and evil. Ladd is a more "aes-thetic" object, with some of the "universality" of a piece of sculpture; his special quality is in his physical smoothness and serenity, unworldly and yet not innocent, but suggesting that no experience can really touch him. Stevens has tried to freeze the Western myth once and for all in the immobility of Alan Ladd's countenance. If *Shane* were "right," and fully successful, it might be possible to say there was no point in making any more Western movies; once the hero is apotheosized, variation and development are closed off.

Shane is not "right," but it is still true that the possibilities of fruitful variation in the Western movie are limited. The form can keep its freshness through endless repetitions only because of the special character of the film medium, where the physical difference between one object and another—above all, between one actor and another—is of such enormous importance, serving the function that is served by the variety of language in the perpetuation of literary types. In this sense, the "vocabulary" of films is much larger than that of literature and falls more readily into pleasing and significant arrangements. (That may explain why the middle levels of excellence are more easily reached in the movies than in literary forms, and perhaps also why the status of the movies as art is constantly being called into question.) But the advantage of this almost automatic particularity belongs to all films alike. Why does the Western movie especially have such a hold on our imagination?

Chiefly, I think, because it offers a serious orientation to the problem of violence such as can be found almost nowhere else in our culture. One of the well-known peculiarities of modern civilized opinion is its refusal to acknowledge the value of violence. This refusal is a virtue, but like many virtues it involves a certain willful blindness and it encourages hypocrisy. We train ourselves to be shocked or bored by cultural images of violence, and our very concept of heroism tends to be a passive one: we are less drawn to the brave young men who kill large number of our enemies than to the heroic prisoners who endure torture without capitulating. In art, though we may still be able to understand and participate in the values of the Iliad, a modern writer like Ernest Hemingway we find somewhat embarrassing: there is no doubt that he stirs us, but we cannot help recognizing also that he is a little childish. And in the criticism of popular culture, where the educated observer is usually under the illusion that he has nothing at stake, the presence of images of violence is often assumed to be in itself a sufficient ground for condemnation.

These attitudes, however, have not reduced the element of violence in our culture but, if anything, have helped to free it from moral control by letting it take on the aura of "emancipation." The celebration of acts of violence is left more and more to the irresponsible: on the higher cultural levels to writers like Céline, and lower down to Mickey Spillane or Horace McCoy, or to the comic books, television, and the movies. The gangster movie, with its numerous variations, belongs to this cultural "underground" which sets forth the attractions of violence in the face of all our higher social attitudes. It is a more "modern" genre than the Western, perhaps even more profound, because it confronts industrial society on its own ground—the city—and because, like much of our advanced art, it gains its effects by a gross insistence on its own narrow logic. But it is anti-social, resting on fantasies of irresponsible freedom. If we are brought finally to acquiesce in the denial of these fantasies it is only because they have been shown to be dangerous, not because they have given way to a better vision of behavior.[2]

In war movies, to be sure, it is possible to present the uses of violence within a framework of responsibility. But there is the disadvantage that modern war is a co-operative enterprise; its violence is largely impersonal, and heroism belongs to the group more than to the individual. The hero of a war movie is most often simply a leader, and his superiority is likely to be expressed in a denial of the heroic: you are not supposed to be brave, you are supposed to get the job done and stay alive (this too, of course, is a kind of heroic posture, but a new—and "practical"—one). At its best, the war movie may represent a more

---

2. I am not concerned here with the actual social consequences of gangster movies, though I suspect they could not have been so pernicious as they were thought to be. Some of the compromises introduced to avoid the supposed bad effects of the old gangster movies may be, if anything, more dangerous, for the sadistic violence that once belonged only to the gangster is now commonly enlisted on the side of the law and thus goes undefeated, allowing us (if we wish) to find in the movies a sort of "confirmation" of our fantasies.

civilized point of view than the Western, and if it were not continually marred by ideological sentimentality we might hope to find it developing into a higher form of drama. But it cannot supply the values we seek in the Western.

Those values are in the image of a single man who wears a gun on his thigh. The gun tells us that he lives in a world of violence, and even that he "believes in violence." But the drama is one of self-restraint: the moment of violence must come in its own time and according to its special laws, or else it is valueless. There is little cruelty in Western movies, and little sentimentality; our eyes are not focused on the sufferings of the defeated but on the deportment of the hero. Really, it is not violence at all which is the "point" of the Western movie, but a certain image of man, a style, which expresses itself most clearly in violence. Watch a child with his toy guns and you will see: what most interests him is not (as we so much fear) the fantasy of hunting others, but to work out how a man might look when he shoots or is shot. A hero is one who looks like a hero.

Whatever the limitations of such an idea in experience, it has always been valid in art, and has a special validity in an art where appearances are everything. The Western hero is necessarily an archaic figure; we do not really believe in him and would not have him step out of his rigidly conventionalized background. But his archaicism does not take away from his power; on the contrary, it adds to it by keeping him just a little beyond the reach both of common sense and of absolutized emotion, the two usual impulses of our art. And he has, after all, his own kind of relevance. He is there to remind us of the possibility of style in an age which has put on itself the burden of pretending that style has no meaning, and, in the midst of our anxieties over the problem of violence, to suggest that even in killing or being killed we are not freed from the necessity of establishing satisfactory modes of behavior. Above all, the movies in which the Westerner plays out his role preserve for us the pleasures of a complete and self-contained drama—and one which still effortlessly crosses the boundaries which divide our culture—in a time when other, more consciously serious art forms are increasingly complex, uncertain, and ill-defined.

John Ford

Peter Bogdanovich

[The noted film director, John Ford, has probably done as much as anyone to popularize the Western film. His Westerns, which include *The Iron Horse* (1924), *Stage Coach* (1939), *My Darling Clementine* (1946), *Fort Apache* (1948), *The Searchers* (1956), and *The Man Who Shot Liberty Valance* (1962), have won praise as the highest art of the American cinema. Ford was always aware of the history of the real West, and his films contain actual locations and realistic settings. However, Ford freely admitted that he shaped his West according to what he considered the nation's need for heroic figures. In this section of a monograph and interview by Peter Bogdanovich (now a noted director in his own right), John Ford's not always consistent attitude toward Western films is presented and analyzed.]

Ford's work, like his personality, is filled with ambiguities. "When the legend becomes fact," says a newspaper editor near the end of *Liberty Valance,* "print the legend." And this in a film that has just *exposed* a legend: Stoddard, famous as "the man who shot Liberty Valance," has finally told the truth: it was Doniphon who actually killed the notorious outlaw. "Print the legend." Ford prints the fact. In *Fort Apache,* Col Thursday (Henry Fonda) underestimates his Indian opponent and arrogantly leads his men into a massacre. But, at the end, the newspapers—with the help of those Army men who witnessed the spectacle— are writing the birth of a legend, creating a noble leader who died with his men. Yet Ford has just shown us the facts: Thursday was wrong; his men died in vain. On the other hand—and here is a further level of meaning—Ford is saying that the Cavalry, in fact the country, lives on despite the errors of any one leader; and if printing a falsehood will help the morale of the Cavalry or the nation— then print the legend.

But Ford, never dogmatic, has also shown us the truth. . . . Ford's sympathies have always been with the outsider, the dispossessed. The homeless Indians of *Cheyenne Autumn* are not far removed from the wandering Oakies of *The Grapes of Wrath.*

In his desire not to be typed "a Western director" (it is revealing that he waited ten years before making his first sound western, *Stagecoach*), Ford has been versatile through his career, and many of his finest pictures are far removed from that genre: *They Were Expendable, The Quiet Man, The Long Gray Line, The Wings of Eagles, The Last Hurrah.* Yet he has made more of them than anything else, and his personality is most clearly reflected in his westerns: to follow their mood since 1950, for example, is to see a key progression. Having

From **John Ford** by Peter Bogdanovich. Originally published by the University of California Press; reprinted by permission of The Regents of the University of California.

reached the height of optimism in *Wagon Master,* that most inspiring story of pioneer spirit, Ford completed his cavalry trilogy (in the same year) with *Rio Grande,* a film that mingled feelings of loss (the Civil War—the burning of the Shenandoah Valley) with the glorified charges of the Apache wars. His next western, made six years later, showed the beginning of a change: an epic story, filled with comedy and drama, *The Searchers* nonetheless ends on a tragic note as the man of the West goes off alone. *The Horse Soldiers, Sergeant Rutledge* and *Two Rode Together* are increasingly bitter in spirit, until with *The Man Who Shot Liberty Valance* (his most important film of the sixties), he seems to be making his final statement on the western. (The subsequent "Wild West" interlude in *Cheyenne Autumn* is treated as farce—the Wyatt Earp he glorified in *My Darling Clementine* has become a wily joker.) Doniphon, the epitome of the Old West, dies without his boots on, without his gun, and receives a pauper's funeral, but the man of the New West, the man of books, has ridden to success on the achievements of the first, who was discarded, forgotten. It is perhaps the most mournful, tragic film Ford has made. There is nothing wrong with the New West—it was inevitable; yet as they ride back East, Stoddard and Hallie look out of their train window at the passing western landscape and Hallie comments on how untamed it used to be, and how it has changed, almost into a garden. But one feels that Ford's love, like Hallie's, remains with the wildness of the cactus rose. . . .

Part of an Interview

In Fort Apache, *do you feel the men were right in obeying Fonda even though it was obvious he was wrong and they were killed because of his error?*
Yes—he was the Colonel, and what he says—goes; whether they agree with it or not—it still pertains. In Vietnam today, probably a lot of guys don't agree with their leader, but they still go ahead and do the job.
The end of Fort Apache *anticipates the newspaper editor's line in* Liberty Valance, *"When the legend becomes a fact, print the legend." Do you agree with that?*
Yes—because I think it's good for the country. We've had a lot of people who were supposed to be great heroes, and you know damn well they weren't. But it's good for the country to have heroes to look up to. Like Custer—a great hero. Well, he wasn't. Not that he was a stupid man—but he did a stupid job that day. Or Pat Garrett, who's a great Western hero. He wasn't anything of the sort—supposed to have shot Billy the Kid—but actually one of his posse did. On the other hand, of course, the legend has always had some foundation.
Is the line in Fort Apache, *"I can't see them anymore—all I can see is the flags,"* *meant to be symbolic?*
More as a slight touch of premonition about her husband's death. It was very funny—she said the line, and another actress said, "You misread that—you should say, 'All I can see *are* the flags.' "

[There have been at least five major biographical films on William Bonney—*Billy the Kid* (1930), *Billy the Kid* (1941), *The Outlaw* (1946), *The Left-Handed Gun* (1957), and *Pat Garrett and Billy the Kid* (1973). Reprinted in this section are some of the critical reactions to the original Billy the Kid film, starring ex-football hero, Johnny Mack Brown. Most interesting of these reactions is that of the film's director, King Vidor, who claimed he wanted to tell at least some of the real story of William Bonney, but was convinced that audiences would never accept it.]

Billy the Kid

Ralph A. Lynd
(Glendale California News Press, December 2, 1930)

When MGM decided to glorify Billy the Kid in the picture of that name they evidently chased the staff of the research department off the lot and turned the task over to someone whose one idea of a western thriller is a composite of gunshots and gooey romance and who was also unhampered by any respect for established fact or even for inherent probabilities.

The picture, "Billy the Kid," playing at the Glendale this week, is in few ways the story of the actual range killer.

The studio officials, pleasing the tastes of their followers, have made instead a pleasing, heroic story, using the great scenic backgrounds of New Mexico and bare thread of the real story as a basis.

Billy the Kid blazed a gory trail in New Mexico. He is reported to have done his first killing when he was a boy of 12 in Silver City, after which he vanished from his New Mexico haunts until he reached his maturity.

He returned with a record as a killer that won him a place among the professional gunmen who were enlisted on the opposing sides of the Lincoln county war that turned that section of New Mexico into a shambles for several years.

How many victims fell before Billy the Kid's blazing guns no one can say accurately. Old timers in New Mexico who knew the Kid in his heyday claim that he had lost count of the number of Mexicans he had shot down, while the Americans, good and bad, who fell before his deadly aim were placed in excess of a score.

So far as the rattle of artillery fire in the picture is concerned the showing runs true to the accepted and established form of Billy the Kid.

But his romantic interludes, so far as history tells us, never brought him in contact with anyone outside the purlieus of the towns that fringed the Rio Grande.

The fight in the McKeen home, as shown in the picture, keeps fairly close to the known facts, as does his shooting of Ballinger and his escape from the Lincoln county jail.

From the motion picture **Billy the Kid**. Courtesy of United Artists 16.

His conference with General Lew Wallace is also fairly close to fact, although the record does not show that he paraded down the main street of Lincoln between lines of saluting troopers, to the fanfare of a bugle.

Billy the Kid was a cold-blooded killer, whose only redeeming feature was the chilled steel courage of his caste.

To place him on a pedestal and present him as a factor in the bringing of law and order to the southwest is a joke to anyone who knows anything of his history.

Another inconsistency of the play is the casting of Johnny Mack Brown, a good looking youth with a broad Alabama accent, for the role of a buck-toothed New York slum product.

Honesty or Hokum —
Which Does the Public Want?

Elena Boland

(*Los Angeles Times,* November 2, 1930)

King Vidor is "through" fighting for pictures that are "honest."
The director who turned out "The Big Parade," "The Crowd," and
"Hallelujah," who has pioneered for what he calls realism on the screen, is from
now on "going to give the public only what it wants."

Furthermore, he is quite sure this decision is not a moment's whim.
Perhaps he will change his mind later, and perhaps he won't. At least he is
positive in his stand now.

"What's the use of trying to make pictures the way you want them?" he
declared. "What's the use of fighting for what you think is right? Put honesty on
the screen and no one will believe it. Life is too short to battle with ignorance;
the ignorance of the masses for whom pictures are made. So I give up. I'll give
the public what it wants and let it go at that."

But Vidor, the pioneer, does not despair. Some day, he declares, he will
have his own studio, there to take his time and do what he wants. In the
meantime he will settle down to the business of catering to the public; and
taking that for what it is, he won't complain. And, perhaps, he will surprise
himself with some pretty good pictures—for the public.

"The pictures I would make to suit myself," he explains, "probably no
one would come to see, except a few of my friends. But they would be stories of
life and real people and would be told the way they actually happened.
Hollywood won't let you do that. Hollywood is a rut, a money-mad rut that
sucks you in and stamps you. One has to realize this and escape. I want to go far
away and learn about things we know nothing of here, strange places and strange
tales; then I'll bring them back and make them into pictures—my way."

Vidor's farewell gesture to the cause of realism and truth is the story of
"Billy the Kid," which he has retold on the Criterion screen. It is a story of
adventures so incredible that to many Vidor experts they will appear far-fetched
fantasies of the studio. But the truth is that each of the miraculous escapes
which are portrayed is an authentic reproduction of one of the notorious
bandit's escapades. The superb boldness of this youthful killer, who had shot
down twenty-one men before he himself was destroyed at the age of 21,
together with the paradoxical qualities of his character, has held King Vidor's
interest over several years.

" . . . The picture as it stands finished is not what it was originally.
Censorship and public opinion necessitated changes.

"Of course, we had to clean it up somewhat to begin with," explained Vidor, "but we stuck to the historical ending, the death of Billy. Well, when we previewed it we found that the audience didn't want him to die. So we fixed it so that he would live, and to do that meant that we had to go back through the entire story, changing it so that it would appear justifiable that he should not die. You see, the public doesn't want the truth. Why should I try any more to give it to them?"

From the motion picture **Billy the Kid**. Courtesy of United Artists 16.

From the motion picture **The Left-Handed Gun.**
Copyright © 1958 by Warner Bros. Pictures, Inc.

Geronimo

[The prototype savage Indian of Western movies has always been Geronimo. Although the real Geronimo never led more than a small band of renegades, and was a short, rather meek-looking man, his movie counterpart is traditionally the personification of an evil, subhuman savage. In 1939 Paramount Pictures released a frightening Western called *Geronimo,* which did much to reinforce the ferocious savage stereotype of the Indian. Reprinted in this section is some of Paramount's original sensationalistic promotion of the film, including a specially prepared "classroom guide" for American history students on the bravery of the cavalry in Indian wars. Also included here is a typical review of the film and a tongue-in-cheek article on its Indian actors.]

Vivid Action-Movie at the Paramount

Kate Cameron

(*New York Daily News,* February 8, 1940)

Not since Walter Wanger's production of "Stagecoach" faded from the screens hereabouts have theatre audiences experienced the breathless excitement that Paramount's "Geronimo" engenders. The Injun film was presented at the Paramount Theatre yesterday to the delight of an audience that thrilled audibly to the gory action.

As a screen thriller, "Geronimo" serves its purpose well by giving us an exciting and bloody account of the last of the Indian wars. But as a historical record of the life and times of the fierce Apache chief, Geronimo, who worried the United States Army and the pioneers who crossed the continent in processions of covered wagons, it is somewhat inaccurate and ludicrously off the mark at its trumped-up conclusion.

There is enough fast and furious movement among the characters to satisfy the most rapacious action fan. The time is the middle 80s, a decade after Gen. Custer made his last stand against the Sioux Indians in the North. The place is the rocky hills and plains of Arizona, where Geronimo and his bands of wild Apaches surprised and attacked travelers and played a treacherous game of hide-and-seek with Gen. Steele and the cavalry.

Chief Thunder Cloud, who is a full blooded Cherokee, plays Geronimo with real conviction. The personal conflict between the stern disciplinarian, Gen. Steele, and his young son, who is sent to his father's command by President Grant, is reminiscent of the drama of "Lives of a Bengal Lancer." Ralph Morgan, in the role of the father, and William Henry, as Lieut. Steele, are somewhat less than convincing, especially in their last scene together. Gene Lockhart gives a very poor imitation of a coward, as the treacherous white man who sells arms to the Indians. Preston Foster, in the role of a courageous officer, and Andy Devine as a scout attached to the Army, are excellent.

Only As Bad As They're Painted

John del Valle

(*New York Herald Tribune*, February 4, 1940)

Hollywood.—An Indian, it may be said with assurance, is not always as bad as he is painted, particularly if he is done up by a movie makeup man. If he holds a card with the Screen Actors Guild, his savagery is for pay, and when he goes on the warpath it is because it's in the script. This place has become the happy hunting grounds, the aboriginal redskin is growing soft, and persuading the Hollywood Indian to put vim in his villainy is a feat.

Such has been the case in the cinema's re-enactment of the Apache uprising of the 1870s, a series of raids and massacres which was not quelled until the United States government, at a cost of some $70,000,000, captured Chief Geronimo and ended his depredations. Titled "Geronimo!" the picture derives its name from its menace, a character portrayed by the normally benign Chief Thunder Cloud of the Cherokee nation.

Thunder Cloud is an example of the debilitation that is Hollywood. Fine, sturdy fellow though he is, with warrior build and the stamina of his forebears, Thunder Cloud prides himself on his baritone voice of possible operatic caliber and on intellectual attainments not in keeping with tribal traditions. A university graduate, he makes a continuing study of the anthropology of his people.

Thunder Cloud got the role because he resembles the late Geronimo and can act. This latter quality is unusual; Indians ordinarily are not adept in the finer nuances of portrayal. Jim Thorpe is an exception who proves the rule; Thunder Cloud now shares the distinction.

But much as he wanted the role, Thunder Cloud went into open rebellion against being made too much of a villain. He called attention to the fact that he also plays Tonto, a "good Indian," in the Lone Ranger series, and has quite a following among the younger set. He didn't want to disillusion them.

Director Paul Sloan made him one concession. He agreed to delete a scene of "Geronimo" showing the Chief scalping a defenseless white woman.

"If I did a scene like that," said the Chief, "every child in America would hate me."

Thunder Cloud's countenance was found to be just a little too much on the side of nobility, too little on the side of evil, so the makeup men went to work on him. Guided by photographs of Geronimo, they altered his mouth line to make it grimmer, built up the bridge of his nose a touch, and traced deep lines in his cheeks. The resultant visage, they concluded, should bring out the cold shivers.

Much of the picture was shot on location, but some footage was filmed in and about the studio and the Hollywood Indian colony, perhaps the largest group of redskins not on a government reservation, was called on for extra players.

The common garden variety of Indian extra earns $8.25 a day when afoot, with feathered headdress, breech clout, moccasins and implements of war supplied by the studio; $11 a day when on horseback. This is wampum in any dialect. And the Indian extra who can supply his own accouterments draws $13.75 a day.

Occasional controversy arises over whether the Indian extras are to apply their own war paint, or have it done by studio makeup men. This is complicated by the fact that the Indian's own clay and herbal pigments frequently will not suffice, being unphotogenic and often representative of some tribe foreign to the story.

Early in the shooting of "Geronimo!" the question came to a head.

"My people," said Thunder Cloud, "wish to apply their own war paint."

He explained to Sloan that war painting was an esoteric art, not understood by the paleface makeup man, that every line meant something, that one Indian was entitled to put a ring of red on his left wrist because he had been shot there and another to cover himself with yellow horse shoes because he had been kicked by a palomino horse.

"Okay," said Sloan. "Let 'em paint themselves—but we'll provide the paint so it'll show on the screen."

This recalled a lamentable occurrence some years ago when a film company was making pictures in the Apache territory. The director gave the Indians a small barrel of roofing paint from the property wagon. The braves laid it on thick from head to foot, and their war dance was a huge success.

But at midnight the paint refused to come off. The Indians began rubbing themselves against rocks, with cries of despair. The director and his technical crew decided to leave that place hurriedly.

Geronimo

(Studio Advertisement, Paramount, 1940)

"See thousands of yelling savages hurl themselves
    against a ring of deadly steel!"

"See the death-defying race of the ammunition wagon
    through 10,000 yelling redskins!"

"See two hardy frontier fighters withstand
    the fiendish tortures of the war-mad Geronimo!"

"Deadlier'n a rattler and twice as slippery—
    that's Geronimo!"—Andy Devine, that old Indian fighter

[Chief Thunder Cloud in the title role was unbilled]

Geronimo

(Educational Promotion)

Cash in on the historical angle with schools and special groups:

Schools—Crash classrooms with these promotion ideas, which are in the safe and sane tradition desired by the faculty. Here are suggestions for pertinent subjects in the curriculum. Use passes as rewards.

> *History Classes*—Set up a still display to give youngsters background for an essay contest and an appetite for the box office. The topic: *Geronimo! The Last Savage.*

> *Manual Training Classes*—Have the boys build model Indian canoes. These will make practical ashtrays after they have been judged. A "Geronimo" tomahawk is a second idea, but teachers will probably favor the first.

> *Art Classes*—Students may compete in a contest calling for drawing a color portrait of Geronimo. In this case supply stills for class display and consultation.

> *Domestic Science Classes*—Girls may compete producing the best originally designed Indian rug or blanket.

Local Indian Fighters—Your community can probably produce one or two old veterans who fought in some of the Indian wars. Find them and enlist their aid in selling "Geronimo!" Get their reactions and quote them in advance advertising. Try to plant a local feature story based on the experiences of the veterans and be sure to have them refer prominently to Geronimo as the most brutal savage of them all. If one of the veterans can carry off a talk, use him as a prologue to the "Geronimo!" trailer.

Two Views of Heroism

[Walter Van Tilburg Clark's book, *The Ox-Bow Incident,* is a classic realistic novel about the Old West. Detailing the story of how a group of Nevada cowboys brutally lynch three innocent men by mistake, the novel is a vivid essay against mob violence and prejudice. The tale is seen through the eyes of two amiable young wranglers named Gil Carter and Art Croft, who reluctantly join the mob, but ultimately yield to its pressure and take part in the hanging. At a crucial point in the story, a town shopkeeper who opposes the hanging, Mr. Davies, agrees to have the members of the "posse" vote on whether to postpone it until the accused are tried in court. He hopes to appeal to their civilized senses. The mob's leader, an ex-Confederate officer named Tetley, wants the ballot, feeling the majority will be with him.

The interesting thing about this episode is that although five courageous men (including Tetley's son) vote to stop the lynching, Gil Carter and Art Croft are not among them. Two potential cowboy-heroes are not allowed to be heroic. This is what gives the novel its raw, realistic power.

The film version of *The Ox-Bow Incident* is a respectful adaptation of Clark's novel. The only significant change in the screenplay is in the characterization of Gil Carter. Portrayed by Henry Fonda, Carter *does* vote to postpone the hanging in the crucial scene. His partner, Art, follows him after some hesitation. Hence, the "good" minority trying to stop the hanging in the film consists of seven men, including the traditional Western hero figure. Later in the film, just before the nooses are tightened on the three accused men, Carter tries to stop the lynchings by pulling his gun. Although he is subdued by the mob, the film's Carter gives the audience the kind of heroic figure it would expect in a Western—even one as depressing as this one.

Reprinted here are the "balloting" sections of the novel and the screenplay (by Lamar Trotti) for comparison.]

[THE BALLOT] THE NOVEL

"I think we'd better get this settled," Tetley said. "We must act as a unit in a job like this. Then we need fear no mistaken reprisal. Are you content to abide by a majority decision, Davies?"

Davies looked him in the face, but even that seemed to be an effort. He wouldn't say anything.

"How about the rest of you men?" Tetley asked, "Majority rule?"

There were sounds of assent. Nobody spoke out against it.

"It has to," Ma said. "Among a bunch of pigheads like this you'd never get everybody to agree to anything."

"We'll vote," Tetley said. "Everybody who is with Mr. Davies for putting this thing off and turning it over to the courts, step out here." He pointed to a space among us on the south side of the fire.

Davies walked out there and stood. Nobody else came for a moment, and he flushed when Tetley smiled at him. Then Sparks shambled out too, but smiling apologetically. Then Gerald Tetley joined them. His fists were clenched as he felt the watching, and saw his father's sardonic smile disappear slowly until his face was a stern mask. There was further movement, and some muttering, as Carl Bartlett and Moore stood out with them also. No more came.

"Five," said Tetley. "Not a majority, I believe, Mr. Davies."

He was disappointed that anyone had ventured to support Davies; I'm sure he hadn't expected as many as four others. I know I hadn't. And he was furious that Gerald had been among them. But he spoke quietly and ironically, as if his triumph had been complete.

[THE BALLOT] THE SCREENPLAY

Shot 179—Closeup (Tetley looking off at Davies)

TETLEY: (impatiently) "Gentlemen, I suggest we act as a unit so there can be no questions of mistaken reprisals. Mr. Davies, are you willing to abide by a majority decision?"

Shot 180—Closeup (Davies as he looks up and off at Tetley and makes no reply)

Shot 181—Group Shot
The men are looking at Davies, waiting. He puts the letter in his pocket.

TETLEY: "How about the rest of you people?"

Voices (Mapes, Farnley, Winder taking lead): "Sure." "Go ahead." "Majority rules."

TETLEY: "Everybody who is with Mr. Davies for putting this thing off and turning it over to the courts, step over here."

And he points to a space in the center of the group. Davies immediately steps forward. There is a slight pause, then Sparks shambles out and joins Davies, smiling apologetically. After another pause, Moore also steps out beside Davies, followed by another man. *Then Gil moves up beside Davies, followed after a moment by Art.* [Italics added by the Editor.]

Shot 182—Closeup (Martin watching, torn between hope and fear)

Shot 183—Closeup (Tetley a faint sardonic smile on his face. Suddenly the smile fades and his face becomes a stern mask.)

Shot 184—Wider Angle (as Gerald Tetley steps into the center beside Davies. His fists are clenched. Seven in all.)

Shot 185—Closeup (Davies as he looks around the circle of faces, a pleading look in his eyes)

Shot 186—Pan Shot (faces)

The men avert their eyes, but no one else responds. Farnley is scowling at the seven men who have dared vote for the law. Monty Smith is taking a drink. Gabe Hart grins stupidly. Ma Grier is looking off at the sky.

Shot 187—Close Shot

TETLEY: (Self-possessed, showing no signs of weariness or excitement) "Seven. Not a majority, I believe, Mr. Davies."

FOR DISCUSSION

1. Cinema historians Fenin and Everson indicate that Hollywood has used historical themes rather carelessly as background for many Westerns. Why has a peculiarly American film genre like the Western shown such a lack of respect for even the surface facts of American history? Are elements of the typical horse-opera-like action, romantic plot, "good" vs. "evil," sufficient reason to distort historical incidents? Why, for example, does the Geronimo of most films die, when the real man lived to write his memoirs? What does the Western movie's lack of respect for history tell us about our own attitudes toward the American past?

2. Robert Warshow analyzes the classical film cowboy as follows: "The Westerner is the last gentleman, and the movies which over and over again tell his story are probably the last art form in which the concept of honor retains its strength." After reading this volume so far, how do you feel about Warshow's comment? Do you believe it? Does it apply to all Western films and literature (even though he would limit it to the "classic" Westerns described in his essay)? What has Warshow's statement in common with the far less sophisticated Gene Autry's "Ten Commandments of the Cowboys"?

3. A famous line in John Ford's *The Man Who Shot Liberty Valance* (a Western that allows its audience to penetrate traditional myth) is "When the legend becomes a fact, print the legend." Ford says he agrees with the statement and claims to have used it as a guide for his Westerns (though, in fact,he hasn't). Do you agree or disagree with Ford's comments that heroic legends are "good for the country"? Explain.

4. In the section on the 1930 screen version of *Billy the Kid,* director King Vidor claimed he wanted at least to have Billy die at the end of the film, but that preview audiences "wouldn't buy that ending." Why do you think audiences in 1930 reacted that way? In later versions of *Billy the Kid,* no matter how whitewashed the character was, at least he died in the famous duel with sheriff Pat Garrett. Was Vidor's decision in 1930 too hasty, or has audience attitude changed since that time? Why would fans of the traditional Western object to the hero's demise, even if that "hero" were a notorious outlaw?

5. What are your reactions to the article entitled "Only As Bad As They're Painted" about the Indian actors in the 1939 film, *Geronimo?* How would Indian social critic, Vine Deloria, Jr. (see pp. 21-27), react to the description of Hollywood's creation of "savage" Indians?

6. Analyze the "balloting sequence" from the screenplay of *The Ox-Bow Incident* and compare it to the same sequence in Walter Van Tilburg Clark's novel. Why has the film version made the characters of Carter and Croft sympathetic? Robert Warshow maintains that the film version of

The Ox-Bow Incident is unique because it has no hero. But it does have heroic identification figures, particularly Henry Fonda as Gil Carter, who does *try* to stop the lynching. Warshow claims "a hero would have to stop the lynching or be killed trying to stop it, and then the 'problem' of the lynching would no longer be central." Why doesn't the film's Gil Carter qualify as a hero under Warshow's code? Does the film's Carter make the "(problem) of the lynching" less "central" than it is in the novel? Why didn't the film-makers merely stick to the novel's characterization?

PART FOUR

The Rise of the Cowboy Anti-Hero—
Trends in Westerns Since 1960

The Western movie has changed significantly since the early 1960s. With the increased popularity of television, the decline of the Hollywood staple "B" pictures, and, perhaps, the greater sophistication of screen audiences, the old-time cowboy picture seems to have finally lost some of its traditional appeal. Western films of the 1960s and 1970s have taken on a cynical, anti-heroic attitude toward the West.

This section is designed to analyze the shifting trends in Western movie mythology. In the first half, critical appraisals of recent Westerns note changing developments in the genre and analyze whether these films are any better than their earlier counterparts. The second half of this section concentrates on a few individual examples of "revisionist" Westerns, which are deliberately designed to destroy the previous myths of heroic cowboy literature and films—particularly *The Wild Bunch, Doc,* and Arthur Kopit's play *Indians.*

Cowboys, Movies, Myths, and Cadillacs: Realism in the Western

Larry McMurtry

In 1961 I published a novel with cowboys in it, in 1963 it was made into the movie *Hud,* and ever since then people have been asking me if I think movies and television portray the American cowboy as he really is. I think, of course, that they do not, and personally I have no great desire to see them try. My questioners apparently assume that realism in movies is something more than a method; for them it is a kind of moral imperative. In their view documentary similitude equals truth, equals art, and the western should quit falsifying and become a responsible genre.

From **Man and the Movies,** edited by W. R. Robinson in **The American West on Film.** Reprinted by permission of the publishers, Louisiana State University Press.

For my part, fond as I am of responsible genres, I am not at all sure I want the western to be one. Until I read Robert Warshow's celebrated essay on the westerner, I had been quite content to think of the western simply as a mode of entertainment, a mode in which the only "real" things were the horses and the landscape. I used westerns . . . as a means of disengaging myself from life for a couple of hours. I am seldom in the mood to look down my nose at such a cheap, convenient escape, and even seldomer in the mood to wonder whether the escape is art. I identify easily, and if I go to a movie that is even slightly real I am apt to find myself more engaged with life than ever; if it is a great movie the engagement may result in a sense of purgation, but great movies are few and far between, and if the film is all-too-believable and only middling good I often regret that I didn't choose a western.

The kind of escapes one chooses is significant, no doubt, but our culture provides such a variety that one's curiosity about them is apt to be somewhat blunted. Until *Hud* was made I had never thought much about the western as art, but it had dawned on me that there was a certain lack of similitude in Hollywood's treatment of cowboy life. Now and then, watching a western, I would see evidence that some director had got together with his technical adviser and made an earnest attempt to get his actors to looking like so-called "real" cowboys; the result, usually, was pretty much mixed pickles, with a few good details overbalanced by numerous examples of ignorance, negligence, or disinterest. In the interests of particularity I might point out three actions that are almost never performed on the screen as they would be on the range. Screen cowboys usually hold their bridle reins in their fists, as if they were gripping bouquets of flowers, whereas range cowboys normally control them with thumb, index finger, and middle finger. Second, screen cowboys spur their horses behind the girths, working cowboys forward of the girths and sometimes as high as the shoulders. Finally, there is the trotting-cattle syndrome, a recurrent screen phenomenon. The moviegoer usually sees cattle being driven across the screen at a pace so rapid that even the wiriest longhorn could not sustain it the length of Hollywood Boulevard without suffering a collapse; the great trail herds of the 1870s and 1880s were eased and grazed along at a sedate eight to ten miles a day. Since they often had to go all the way from Texas to Kansas (or in some cases even Montana), anything faster would have been economically disastrous.

Warshow, of course, was right in pointing out that the working cowboy has never been very important in the western movie. The gunfighter has been the central figure, and, as numerous historical narratives point out, cowboys and gunfighters were rather different breeds, neither being very good at the other's specialties. A western may start out with a cowboy hero, but nine times out of ten the plot will require him to become a gunfighter before the end of the film. Recently, there have been signs that this is changing, especially on television. The domestic western is becoming more and more popular (*Bonanza, The Big Valley,* even, I should say, *Gunsmoke*), whereas TV's most impressive old-style gunfighter, Paladin, is seen no more.

At any rate, in citing discrepancies in Hollywood's treatment of cowboy life I did not mean to imply that directors of westerns should get my list and rigorously eliminate trotting cattle and bridle reins held like bouquets. The effectiveness of the western as a genre has scarcely depended upon fidelity of detail or, for that matter, upon emotional validity. Hollywood surely would have been foolish to attempt to do the American cowboy or the winning of the West realistically; applying an anti-romantic technique to an essentially romantic subject would have amounted to a sort of alchemical reverse English; it would have been deliberately turning gold into lead. The cowboy (or the gunfighter), whatever he may be like in real life, lives in the American imagination as a mythic figure, or at least a figure of high romance; his legend, however remotely it may relate to his day-to-day existence, is still one of the most widely compelling of our diminishing number of national legends. Not even kids want to be Indians anymore, and only kids want to be soldiers. The myth of the noble redman is kaput, and the myth of the American poor boy, though it may linger on in figures like Robert E. Lee Prewitt, has lost most of its appeal. Johnny Reb and Billy Yank have faded out; G. I. Joe will follow. The jazzman's appeal has always been too precious, and the teen-ager's, I hope, will always be too teen-age. There are movie stars, sports kings, and rock and roll singers, but here legends tend to accrue around the individual, not around the type. The cowboy, however, absorbed the more general figure of the pioneer or frontiersman, and so far has held his own.

From the motion picture **Hud**. Courtesy of Films Inc.—Paramount Pictures.

The appeal cannot last forever, of course: a good mythic figure must be susceptible of being woven into the national destiny, and since the West definitely has been won the cowboy must someday fade. Indeed, a certain change has already taken place, and was taking place when Warshow wrote his essay (1954). If one can properly apply to the western the terminology which Northrop Frye develops in his essay on fictional modes, we might say that in the 1950s the western (or at least the "serious" western, the only kind Warshow considers) was working its way down from the levels of myth and romance toward the ironic level which it has only recently reached. Westerns like *Shane, The Searchers,* and *Warlock* are in the high mimetic mode; the hero is still superior to other men and to his environment. In *The Gunfighter* this is not the case and we are in the low mimetic mode, just as we are in *Hud.* The latter, indeed, approaches the ironic mode, and we have recently seen an actor (Lee Marvin) win an oscar for a role that parodies the figure of the gunfighter. No doubt high mimetic westerns will continue to be made as long as John Wayne is acting—he wouldn't fit in any other mode—but in number they are declining. The last ten years have witnessed a very sharp drop-off in the production of B and C westerns of the kind that were a Saturday afternoon staple during the 1940s. It is clear that the figure of the westerner is being replaced by more modern figures, principally that of the secret agent. In time, of course, we can expect to see the conquest of space (if we really conquer it) take over the place in the American mythos now held by the winning of the West, but that day has not come. If one agrees with Warshow—and I do—that the western has maintained its hold on our imagination because it offers an acceptable orientation to violence, then it is easy to see why the secret agent is so popular just now. An urban age demands an urban figure; the secret agent, like the westerner a sort of insider-outsider, is an updated type of gunfighter. The secret agent has appropriated the style of the gunfighter and has added urbanity and cosmopolitanism. Napoleon Solo and Matt Dillon both work for the betterment of civilization, but the man from U.N.C.L.E. makes the marshal seem as old-fashioned and domestic as Fibber McGee and Molly. To be widely acceptable, the violence must be satisfactorily aestheticized and brought into line with the times. If only there are some bad Indians out there in space, on a planet we need, then eventually the spaceman's hour will come.

The cowboy's golden age was the last third of the nineteenth century, and Hollywood has been fairly effective in its treatment of the ending of the golden age. The treatment had already begun when Warshow wrote his essay (indeed, it provided him most of his examples—*The Gunfighter, Shane,* and *High Noon*) and has been extended, perhaps most successfully in the excellent sequence of westerns Kirk Douglas has made (*Gunfight at the OK Corral, Last Train from Gun Hill, Lonely Are the Brave*). What happened in the West after the age ended has yet to be dealt with, though a picture such as *Hud* is a beginning.

Hud, a twentieth-century westerner, is a gunfighter who lacks both guns and opponents. The land itself is the same—just as powerful, just as impris-

From the motion picture **Gunfight at OK Corral.**
Courtesy of United Artists 16.

oning—but the social context has changed so radically that Hud's impulse to violence has to turn inward on himself and his family. Hud Bannon is wild in a well-established tradition of western wildness that involves drinking, gambling, fighting, fast and reckless riding and/or driving (Hud has a Cadillac), and, of course, seducing. The tradition is not bogus; the character is pretty much in line with actuality. The cowboy, on screen and off, has generally been distinguished for his daring and his contempt of the middle-class way of life (he remains acutely conscious of the mores of his peers). Though nowadays most cowboys are solidly middle-class in their values, the values sit more lightly on them than on their white-collar cousins.

Hud, of course, is not simply a cowboy; if he were, he could never afford the Cadillac. It is his gun, in a sense, and he can afford it because he is the son of a well-to-do rancher, and a wheeler in his own right. Cowboys and ranchers differ primarily in their economic resources: a rancher is a cowboy who, through some combination of work, luck, judgment, or inheritance, has made good. To a rancher a Cadillac has a dual usefulness, just as the gunfighter's gun once had: it is an obvious and completely acceptable status symbol, and also it is capable of making the long, high-speed drives that are frequently necessary in cattle country; it will do the work. The cowboy proper could no more afford Hud's car than he could afford Hud's women, though granted the latter might vary considerably in expensiveness. In spite of his reputation for going on wild binges the cowboy has usually had to accustom himself to rather Spartan living conditions; indeed, there has always been an element of asceticism in the cowboy's makeup, though it is an asceticism that has tended to wither rather badly when faced with the continuous blasts of sensuality this century has provided. Even so the cowboy's life has not yet become lush; he still gets by with far fewer creature comforts than most Americans have.

In addition to the wildness, Hud also exhibits other characteristics which are typically cowboy: independence is first among them, then pride, stoicism, directness, restlessness. The cowboy also has his own astringent brand of humor, but I have never seen this touched, either in fiction or on the screen. The cowboy's temperament has not changed much since the nineteenth century, but his world has changed a great deal. It has steadily shrunk. There are no more trail herds, no more wide-open cattle towns; no more is there the vast stretch of unfenced land between Laredo and Calgary. If a cowboy is to be really footloose these days, he must take to the rodeo circuit. Rodeo was given one excellent low-mimetic treatment in *The Lusty Men* (1952), but, except for the rodeo sequence in *The Misfits,* has not been used by the movies. (Television, of course, had *Stoney Burke* for awhile.) The big western ranches are now gradually breaking down into smaller and smaller ranches, and with the advent of pickups and horse trailers it is no longer necessary to spend long weeks on the roundup. The principal effect this has had has been to lessen considerably the isolation of the cowboy, to diminish his sense of himself as a man alone. He is gradually being drawn toward the town.

There will be a very poignant story to be told about the cowboy, should Hollywood care to tell it: the story of his gradual metamorphosis into a suburbanite. The story contains an element of paradox, for the bloated urbanism that makes the wild, free cowboy so very attractive to those already urbanized will eventually result in his being absorbed by his audience. In a sense he has been already: nobody watches TV westerns more avidly than cowboys. Of course in this respect legend and fact had long ago begun to intermingle; nature imitated art, to a degree, and the cowboy, however much he might profess to scorn Hollywood, was secretly delighted to believe the romantic things Hollywood told him about himself. Even in his most golden days the cowboy lived within the emotional limits of the western movie and the hillbilly song. Hud Bannon's West is a sort of new lost frontier, and Hud is one of the many people whose capacities no longer fit his situation. He needs more room and less company, and he is unlikely to get either. Someday the ranches of America will all be Southern California size, and all the cattle, perhaps, will be grown in the great feedlots of the Middle West. The descendants of the trail hands will be driving beer trucks in the suburbs of San Antonio, Dodge City, Cheyenne, and a hundred other towns whose names once held a different sort of promise. By that time Hollywood will have grown tired of parodying the gunfighter, the ironic mode may give way to the mythic and the Lone Ranger ride again. Romance will succeed realism, and Gary Cooper (as in *The Plainsman,* say) will be as remote and appealing a figure of romance as Roland or King Arthur. Hud Bannon, by that time, will have traded in his big pink Caddy and left the ranch forever, to become a secret agent, or an astronaut.

Saddle Sore

El Dorado, The War Wagon, The Way West

Pauline Kael

Recently a young film enthusiast from abroad said, "Someday I'm going to cause a revolution in American movies. I'm going to make a Western that's fair to the Indians." I groaned, because just about every writer and director and star about to make a big Western has explained it that way. And just about every Western one can think of has tried to be "fair" in the sense that the Indians were represented as noble and decent people who were pushed to violence by betrayal—by broken treaties that deprived them of land and food, or, in the usual melodrama, by the treachery of "renegade" whites who sold them guns and whiskey or cheated and manipulated them. In the plot structure, the Indians are almost always the victims, the white men the villains.

Yet that is not how audiences, abroad or here, experience the genre; and each new group of film-makers that sets out to right the movie wrongs done to the Indians probably thinks that they're going to correct a grave injustice— "cause a revolution"—as they make the Western that audiences will experience in the same old way. The mechanism is so simple: King Kong is a lovable creature who, chained and goaded beyond endurance, breaks out into a rampage of indiscriminate destruction; the people in the audience, who are like the people being slaughtered in the movie (Kong even starts his rampage on the theatre audience gathered to look at him), are terrified by the big murderous ape. The fact that they felt sympathy for him only a few minutes before adds to the drama, but does not make them fear him the less. The same mechanism was at work with Karloff as the monster in the original *Frankenstein*—yet producers announce that they're going to make a new kind of monster movie in which the monster will be sympathetic. These movie-makers, too, talking about earlier movies, think only of their fear of the monster; they forget the sympathy built up for him early in the pictures. Yet when they talk about the movies they are going to make, they emphasize the sympathy they are going to build up as if they did not know that this was necessary dramatic preparation for the fear and carnage to follow, which is what dominates their own memories and will dominate memories of their films, too.

As a child, I saw the 1932 movie *Freaks,* in which the circus sideshow attractions—the dwarfs, pinheads, idiots, and maimed creatures—fall upon the beautiful trapeze artist, mutilate her and make her one of themselves; and the sight of any deformity used to bring the movie back to me in nightmares. A few years ago I saw the movie again and was amazed to discover that the freaks were meant to be sympathetic and the trapeze artist was a bitch. But I don't think that the director, Tod Browning, who also directed some of the best of the Lon Chaney pictures—and his horribly maimed phantoms and hunchbacks were also meant-to-be-sympathetic—can have been so naive. When tiny, deformed creatures are swarming all over the screen on a mission of mutilation, surely the intention is to terrify us. They are good people who have been mistreated and driven to take direct action only in the preparatory dramatic stages, until they are needed for the climactic fearful images.

In the Western, once we are in danger—huddled in the wagon train with the stars and young lovers and old comics, the arrows coming at us, piercing flesh and starting fires that are burning us alive—the Indians circling us are no longer noble victims. Painted, half-naked men who do not speak our language, who do not know that we mean them no harm, might as well be another species. And decent liberal movie-makers will go on congratulating themselves on their sympathetic treatment of the Indians; and new movie-makers will arrive to show us how to do it all over again.

In some Westerns, cruel and mercenary white men torture and kill Indians—as in *Nevada Smith*, where the hero, Steve McQueen, is half Indian. White men raised as Indians (*Hombre*), white men who have married Indians (*Duel at Diablo, The Way West*), and half-Indian heroes may become almost as popular in our Westerns as the half-Jewish heroes of recent American novels, and for the same reason: the authors hope for extra perspective by playing it both ways. (Traditionally second- and third-generation Jews acted cowboys, first-generation Jews acted Indians; now half-Jews can be half-Indians.) Split in his loyalties, the half-and-half hero can observe the cruelties and misunderstandings of both sides; he's a double loner—an ideally alienated, masochistic modern hero (like Paul Newman in *Hombre*). Typically, his sympathies are with the Indians, though he generally comes through and acts for the whites. In this, the Western has not changed.

But the mechanism of the movie and how we react to it is very different when it is white men torturing Indians. When the murderers are white men, the movie-makers don't feel the guilty necessity to make them sympathetic or to explain them at all; they are simply moral monsters, as in *Nevada Smith*, where the young hero's Indian mother is mutilated—skinned alive—by white degenerates. (This episode is not staged to pleasure the audience or for wanton excitement but rather to make the audience understand the boy's helpless rage. It is violence used to make us hate violence.) And yet their images don't carry the kind of fear that the most meant-to-be-sympathetic Indians do when they turn warlike. We hate the act, but we don't fear the men in the same way. If Hollywood made a movie in which we as audience were involved in the lives of an Indian village which was then attacked by villainous white men, I doubt if we would feel the terror we do when we are attacked by Indians. In general,

Wilhelm Reich was probably right when he said that "a horror story has the same effect whether it deals with Ali Baba and the Forty Thieves or with the execution of white spies. The important thing to the reader is the gooseflesh and not whether it is forty thieves or forty counter-revolutionaries who get decapitated." But suppose it is forty frightening men from some strange tribe whose language and customs we don't understand, or forty Dead End Kids. One raises more gooseflesh than the other. It involves primitive fears—of what we don't know.

There is a fairly widespread assumption that no matter how bad American movies in general are, the Westerns are still great. The people who take this for granted probably don't go to them, but they have an idea that Westerns are authentic movie-making—the *real* movies—and are somehow pure (as Western heroes used to be), exempt from the general corruption. They assume that the Westerns are still there, as pristine and "great" as ever for their kids, as if the air of the wide open spaces would have kept the genre clean.

I don't believe that there ever were the great works in this genre that so many people claim for it. There were some good Westerns, of course, and there was a beautiful kind of purity in some of them, and later even the ritual plots and dull action were, at least, set outdoors, and the horses were often good to look at. But all that was a long time ago. The last good Western that had this ritual purity was Sam Peckinpah's *Ride the High Country,* which came out in 1962. (I am not forgetting David Miller's *Lonely Are the Brave,* which came out at the same time: despite the ingenious and entertaining performance by Walter Matthau and the excellent performance by Kirk Douglas, the Dalton Trumbo script gives the film that awful messagey self-righteousness of *High Noon* and *The Gunfighter* and a fake ironic tragedy, an O. Henry finish—the "last" cowboy is run down by a truck loaded with toilets.) Kids may read the same novel by Robert Louis Stevenson that their parents did, but in movies parents think in terms of the old *Stagecoach* and the kids are going to the new *Stagecoach.* Probably in no art except movies can new practitioners legally eliminate competition from the past. A full-page notice in *Variety* gave warning that Twentieth Century-Fox, which released the 1966 *Stagecoach,* featuring Bing Crosby and Ann-Margret, would "vigorously" prosecute the exhibition of the 1939 original—John Ford's classic Western, one of the most highly regarded and influential movies ever made.

Surely the public should have the right to see the old as well as the new? And not just for its own sake but because that is how we learn about an art. How else do we develop a critical sense about new novels, new paintings, new music, new poetry? If the old is legally retired, we become barbarians (movie barbarians, at least) without a past. The producer of the new version, Martin Rackin, said, "In the process of updating, we can improve on the old films by learning from their mistakes." With equal cynicism, one may reply, "Then why do you remove the old films so that new generations cannot appreciate how much you've improved on them?"

Just about every good Western made since 1939 has imitated *Stagecoach* or has learned something from it. Ironically, the 1966 version merely took the plot and the character stereotypes; and without the simple, clear, epic vision with which John Ford informed them, they are just standard Western equipment. The original *Stagecoach* had a mixture of reverie and reverence about the American past that made the picture seem almost folk art; we *wanted* to believe in it even if we didn't. That is what *Ride the High Country* had, too.

The 1966 *Stagecoach* was undistinguished—a big, brawling action picture that gets audience reactions by brutal fights and narrow escapes photographed right on top of you. The director, Gordon Douglas, doesn't trust you to project yourself imaginatively into his stagecoach; he tries to force you into it—which may make you want to escape to the farthest row in the balcony. Kurosawa[1] (who acknowledges his debt to John Ford) can plunge you into action to make you experience the meaning of action. When the Gordon Douglas crew does it, all it means is they don't want you to get bored. And probably the most that can be said about their movie is that it isn't boring—but then, that could be said of most visits to the dentist. . . .

John Ford himself doesn't bother going outdoors much anymore. A few years back I dragged a painter-friend to see *The Man Who Shot Liberty Valance;* it was a John Ford Western, and though I dreaded an evening with James Stewart and John Wayne, I felt I *should* see it. My friend agreed because "the landscapes are always great"; but after about ten minutes of ugly studio sets, he wanted to leave. By the time Edmond O'Brien, as a drunken newspaper editor, was getting beaten up in the offices of the *Star,* which we saw from inside the glass, my friend was fed up: "Star is rats spelled backward; let's get the hell out of here." What those who believe in the perennial greatness of the Western may not have caught on to is that the new big Western is, likely as not, a studio-set job. What makes it a "Western" is no longer the wide open spaces but the presence of men like John Wayne, James Stewart, Henry Fonda, Robert Mitchum, Kirk Douglas, and Burt Lancaster, grinning with their big new choppers, sucking their guts up into their chests, and hauling themselves onto horses. They are the heroes of a new Western mythology: stars who have aged in the business, who have survived and who go on dragging their world-famous, expensive carcasses through the same old motions. That is the essence of their heroism and their legend. The new Western is a joke and the stars play it for laughs, and the young film enthusiasts react to the heroes not because they represent the mythological heroes of the Old West but because they are mythological movie stars. An actor in his forties would be a mere stripling in a Western these days. Nor would he *belong* in these movies which derive their small, broad humor from the fact that the actors have been doing what they're doing so long

---

1. Akira Kurosawa is a noted Japanese director whose films include **Rashomon** and **Seven Samurai.**

that they're professional Westerners. Like Queen Victoria, John Wayne has become lovable because he's stayed in the saddle into a new era.

The world has changed since audiences first responded to John Wayne as a simple cowboy thirty-seven years ago; now, when he does the same things and represents the same simple values, he's so archaic it's funny. We used to be frightened of a reactionary becoming "a man on horseback"; now that seems the best place for him.

My father went to a Western just about every night of his life that I remember. He didn't care if it was a good one or a bad one or if he'd seen it before. He said it didn't matter. I have just seen three new Westerns—*The Way West, The War Wagon,* and *El Dorado*—and I think I understand what my father meant. If you're going for a Western (the same way you'd sit down to watch a television show), it doesn't much matter which one you see. And if you're going for something else, even the best one of these three isn't good enough. The differences between them aren't, finally, very significant—which is what the mass audience probably understands better than film enthusiasts.

The Way West is about as bad an epic Western as I've ever seen. Students in college film departments sometimes say they can learn more from bad movies than from good ones, because they can examine what the director did wrong: to them *The Way West* should serve as a textbook. Everything essential to explain what's going on seems missing. It's a jerk's idea of an epic: big stars, big landscapes, bad jokes, folksy-heroic music by Bronislau Kaper to plug up the holes, and messy hang-ups. In the neurotic-Western mode, the leader of this 1843 caravan of pioneers, Kirk Douglas, goes in for self-flagellation. (He arranges for his Negro servant to whip him; the darkies have the best rhythm?) Richard Widmark's desire to go West seems to be some sort of compulsive behavior; and Robert Mitchum—the scout!—must be cozened out of irrational mourning for his Indian wife. And to make sure that 1967 audiences won't find this pioneering too old-fashioned, the villainess is a frightened virgin and the heroine is a teen-ager so grotesquely avid for sex that at one point her lusty parents tease that if she doesn't get a husband pretty soon they'll have to mate her with an ox—a line which gets a big laugh. (Maybe it should, because oxen don't mate.) Crude as this movie is, audiences seem to enjoy it; it has that stage-Irish comic sentimentality that used to destroy one's pleasure in many of the John Ford epics and was possibly responsible for their box-office success. *The Way West* was directed by Andrew V. McLaglen, a chip off the old block.

Burt Kennedy's *The War Wagon* is classy Western camp with John Wayne, and Kirk Douglas in a black leather shirt, wearing a ring on his black glove. There are pretty little visual divertissements out of von Sternberg's *Shanghai Gesture* and Buñuel's *L'Age d'Or* and Cocteau's *Orpheus,* and hard-edge cinematography (by William H. Clothier, who also did the more conventional shooting of *The Way West*) that makes the actors look like pop cutouts. The delicate decorator colors include fancy salmon pinks; and there's real bougainvillea growing in the sets. There's even a camp version of backlash when the Indians tell John Wayne that they're not asking him to dinner because having a white man at table offends them. Howard Keel turns up playing an Indian named Levi Walking Bear, and old Bruce Cabot (who saved Fay Wray from King Kong) turns up looking like Maurice Chevalier. And *The War Wagon* has an opening song by Dimitri Tiomkin to tell us it's going to be tough and hardheaded—"All men are fightin' for a wagon full of gold. . . ." In Hollywood that's realistic philosophy.

What does all the chic amount to and who is it for? It's a kind of sophisticated exhibitionism. I received a publicity release from the company that represents *The War Wagon* that puts the movie in more accurate perspective. It's entitled "Suggestions for a Feature" and it reads:

> John Wayne's Western movies are always made in color. In two colors, to be exact: greenback green and glittering gold.
>
> Not a single one of more than 200 films of the great-outdoorsy genre he's made since 1929 has ever lost money. It's a fact of Hollywood life that John Wayne Westerns always show a profit.
>
> For let's face it: John Wayne *is* the Western movie today. Westerns are a folk phenomenon, the one kind of film which has never really fallen from favor, even temporarily. The cinematic years since *The Great Train Robbery* have seen thousands of Western movies, and hundreds of Western heroes. There are scores of them fully and gainfully occupied right this minute, both on theatre and TV screens.
>
> But among them all, there's only one John Wayne. He looms above the others the way the heroes' heads on Mount Rushmore dominate the surrounding pebbles. He may be a homely, middle-aged, battered, unpretentious, non-Actors Studio guy, but he is *the* Western star. And he is undoubtedly going to remain *the* Western star until he's so old he falls off his horse—which will likely be never.
>
> Big John's next big one, *The War Wagon*, is likely to be an especially lucrative lollapalooza. It has the kind of rugged, roisterous script which is the perfect setting for this human diamond-in-the-rough. . . .
>
> We suggest a story on those three phenomenal W's: Westerns, Wayne and *War Wagon*.
>
> It could turn out to be WWWonderful.

That drool contains the awful germy truth: Westerns are money in the bank. When the big studios were breaking up in the fifties and the big box-office stars were forming their own production companies, the Westerns were the safest investment. The studios tried to get whatever money was left in big-name contract stars like Clark Gable and Robert Taylor; and other stars, like Wayne and Douglas and Lancaster, going into business on their own, wanted to protect their investments. That's how the modern Western with the big old stars took over the genre. Others who went into the "safe" genre in the fifties, like Gregory Peck and Frank Sinatra, dropped out (not, I am afraid, from disgust but from financial failure); but Douglas and Lancaster persisted and were joined later by

Robert Mitchum. Soon, because they were so well known anyway and people don't know much about film history, they could pass for real old-time Western heroes, like Wayne.

The structure of this Western-movie business is becoming as feudalistic as the movies themselves: Kirk Douglas has a production company named for his mother (Bryna), another for his son (Joel), yet another for himself and a partner (Douglas-Lewis), etc.; *The War Wagon* is produced by John Wayne's company, Batjac. These corporate-head Westerners appear in each other's films; there are jobs for their sons and their old buddies and the sons of their old buddies. The next big Batjac production is *The Green Berets*, which Wayne himself will direct and one of his sons will produce.

And so we have Kirk Douglas exposing his fat over-muscled chest in *The War Wagon* and doing a series of parodied leaps onto a horse. And for all the aestheticism of dust and hooves and flowers, after a while it might just as well be *The Way West:* when it's the tired comic spectacle of rich old men degrading themselves for more money and fame and power, does it much matter if it's done poorly or with chic? In some ways the chic is more offensive.

The classic Western theme is the doomed hero—the man without a future because the way of life is changing, the frontier is vanishing, and the sheriff and the schoolteacher are representatives of progress and a new order. The hero is the living antique who represents the best of the old order just as it is disappearing. But star-centered movies and TV gave the Westerner a new future: he's got to keep going to keep the series alive. The toilets won't run him down because that would be flushing away good money. Douglas in *The War Wagon* has metamorphosed back into his post-World War II character—the heel. He's now the too smart Westerner, mercenary and untrustworthy in a way the audience is supposed to like. His Westerner is a swinger—a wisecracking fancy talker with intentionally anachronistic modern attitudes.

El Dorado combines Wayne and Mitchum, both looking exhausted. The director, Howard Hawks, is also tired, and like Ford, he doesn't want to go out on location. The theory of why Westerns are such a great form is that directors can show what they can really do in the framework of a ritualized genre and the beauty of the West. But the directors are old and rich, too. (Ford was born in 1895 and directed his first movie in 1917; Hawks was born in 1896 and has been in films since 1918, directing them since the mid-twenties.) Their recent movies look as if they were made for television. Except for a few opening shots, *El Dorado* is a studio job—and it has the second-worst lighting of any movie in recent years (the worst: *A Countess from Hong Kong*). When the movie starts, you have the sense of having come in on a late episode of a TV serial. Mitchum plays a drunken old sheriff (like Charles Winninger in *Destry Rides Again*), and there are home remedies for alcoholism, vomiting scenes that are supposed to be hilarious, and one of those girls who hide their curls under cowboy hats and are mistaken for boys until the heroes start to wrestle with them. Wayne has a beautiful horse in this one—but when he's hoisted onto it and you hear the thud, you don't know whether to feel sorrier for man or beast.

The Old West was a dream landscape with simple masculine values; the code of the old Western heroes probably wouldn't have much to say to audiences today. But the old stars, battling through stories that have lost their ritual meaning, are part of a new ritual that does have meaning. There's nothing dreamy about it: these men have made themselves movie stars—which impresses audiences all over the world. The fact that they can draw audiences to a genre as empty as the contemporary Western is proof of their power. Writers and painters now act out their fantasies by becoming the superstars of their own movies (and of the mass media); Wayne and Douglas and Mitchum and the rest of them do it on a bigger scale. When it makes money, it's not just their fantasy. The heroes nobody believes in—except as movie stars—are the result of a corrupted art form. Going to a Western these days for simplicity or heroism or grandeur or meaning is about like trying to mate with an ox.

The Revisionist Western

[Sam Peckinpah's *The Wild Bunch* (1969) is probably the most controversial Western film ever made. The story of an aging band of outlaws involved in revolutionary Mexico in the early twentieth century (the setting for many "new" Westerns), *The Wild Bunch* was unique because of its portrayal of uncontrolled violence. The film truly has no heroes and its blood-letting is horrifyingly relentless. Obviously, Peckinpah's goal was to shock the old Western legend to death, and this has spurred a great deal of criticism, pro and con. Interestingly, many of the violence techniques of *The Wild Bunch* (including scenes of wholesale killing in slow-motion) have become the stock-in-trade of later Westerns.

Reprinted here are pieces by leading film critics with varying points of view on the film and Peckinpah's "new" West.]

Violence and Beauty Mesh in "Wild Bunch"

Vincent Canby

(*The New York Times,* June 26, 1969)

Sam Peckinpah's *The Wild Bunch* is about the decline and fall of one outlaw gang at what must be the bleeding end of the frontier era, 1913, when Pancho Villa was tormenting a corrupt Mexican Government while the United States watched cautiously from across the border.

The movie, which opened yesterday at the Trans-Lux East and West Theaters, is very beautiful and the first truly interesting American-made Western in years. It's also so full of violence—of an intensity that can hardly be supported by the story—that it's going to prompt a lot of people who do not know the real effect of movie violence (as I do not) to write automatic condemnations of it.

The Wild Bunch begins on a hot, lazy afternoon as six United States soldiers ride into a small Texas border town with all the aloofness of an army of benign occupation. Under a makeshift awning, the good bourgeoisie of San Rafael is holding a temperance meeting. Gentle spinsters, sweating discreetly, vow to abstain from all spirits.

The "soldiers" pass on to the railroad office, which they quietly proceed to rob of its cash receipts. Down the street, a group of children giggle as they watch a scorpion being eaten alive by a colony of red ants. A moment later, the town literally explodes in the ambush that has been set for the outlaws.

Borrowing a device from *Bonnie and Clyde* Peckinpah suddenly reduces the camera speed to slow motion, which at first heightens the horror of the mindless slaughter, and then—and this is what really carries horror—makes it beautiful, almost abstract, and finally into terrible parody.

The audience, which earlier was appalled at the cynical detachment with which the camera watched the death fight of the scorpion, is now in the position of the casually cruel children. The face of a temperance parade marcher erupts in a fountain of red. Bodies, struck by bullets, make graceful arcs through the air before falling onto the dusty street, where they seem to bounce, as if on a trampoline.

This sort of choreographed brutality is repeated to excess, but in excess, there is point, to a film in which realism would be unbearable. *The Wild Bunch* takes the basic element of the Western movie myth, which once defined a simple, morally comprehensible world, and by bending them turns them into symbols of futility and aimless corruption.

The screenplay, by Peckinpah and Walon Green, follows the members of the Wild Bunch from their disastrous, profitless experience at San Rafael to Mexico, where they become involved with a smilingly sadistic Mexican general fighting Villa. Although the movie's conventional and poetic action sequences are extraordinarily good and its landscapes beautifully photographed (lots of dark foregrounds and brilliant backgrounds) by Lucien Ballard, who did *Nevada Smith*, it is most interesting in its almost jolly account of chaos, corruption and defeat. All personal relationships in the movie seem somehow perverted in odd mixtures of noble sentimentality, greed and lust.

Never satisfactorily resolved is the conflict between William Holden, as the aging leader of the Wild Bunch, and Robert Ryan, as his former friend who, with disdain, leads the bounty hunters in pursuit of the gang. An awkward flashback shows the two men, looking like characters out of a silent movie, caught in an ambush in a bordello from which only Holden escapes.

The ideals of masculine comradeship are exaggerated and transformed into neuroses. The fraternal bonds of two brothers, members of the Wild Bunch, are so excessive they prefer having their whores in tandem. A feeling of genuine compassion prompts the climactic massacre that some members of the film trade are calling, not without reason, "the blood ballet."

Peckinpah also has a way of employing Hollywood life to dramatize his legend. After years of giving bored performances in boring movies, Holden comes back gallantly in *The Wild Bunch*. He looks older and tired, but he has style, both as a man and as a movie character who persists in doing what he's always done, not because he really wants the money but because there's simply nothing else to do.

Ryan, Ernest Borgnine and Edmond O'Brien add a similar kind of resonance to the film. O'Brien is a special shock, looking like an evil Gabby Hayes, a foul-mouthed, cackling old man who is the only member of the Wild Bunch to survive.

In two earlier Westerns, *Ride the High Country* (1962) and *Major Dundee* (1965), Peckinpah seemed to be creating comparatively gentle variations on the genre about the man who walks alone—a character about as rare in a Western as a panhandler on the Bowery.

In *The Wild Bunch,* which is about men who walk together, but in desperation, he turns the genre inside out. It's a fascinating movie and, I think I should add, when I came out of it, I didn't feel like shooting, knifing or otherwise maiming any of Broadway's often hostile pedestrians.

Wasn't That Just Lovely,
the Way His Head Exploded?

William Wolf

(*Cue,* August 30, 1969)

Can killing be beautiful? I reject this idea completely. When otherwise astute critics or moviegoers begin talking about scenes of spurting blood, flying flesh, and throats being slashed as having a kind of cinematic beauty because the director does some of it in slow motion, something disturbing is happening to taste and values. Put into the same upsetting category the view that violence piled on in all its gore, without being in a meaningful context, can on its own carry anti-violence implications—especially when the brutality is packaged as get-your-kicks entertainment.

What triggers my dismay is *The Wild Bunch.* The first time I viewed the film I was thoroughly repelled by the orgy of violence, and saw as little reason for discussion of the film as for its having been made. To my total surprise, a number of critics of stature became enthusiastic partisans of the film as a great Western. Some saw it as a brilliant statement against violence. One impassioned reader wrote a well-argued plea for a second viewing on my part.

Determined to discover what ingredients evoked this response, and possibly to have a different reaction the second time around, back I went to endure another few hours of shooting, killing, and blood-spurting directed by Sam Peckinpah, who is now the focal point of a kind of cult. This time I saw it with an evening movie audience at the Trans-Lux East, rather than in a screening room. The experience with an audience was even more dismaying. Formal

Originally published in **Cue**. Reprinted by permission of the author, William Wolf.

criticism is a private matter, not something based on how others react. I have known films I have greatly admired to be ruined by flip audience responses in the wrong places. I have heard audiences laugh up a storm at what I considered the worst drivel. Nevertheless, what was disturbing here was the general, ain't-it-fun vocal response to the brutality. For argument's sake, I will accept the premise that Peckinpah's intent was to show so much violence that one's stomach would be turned against it. He sure as hell wasn't getting any such message across to the more vocal members of this audience—or to me.

I still found the film a poor, run-of-the-mill Western at its core, souped up with an incredible amount of bloody killing and a few stabs at an arty look. I even disagree with those who say the film is well done. Yes, there are some scenes of composition beautiful from a cinematic viewpoint. So what? Good-looking films are routine these days. Unless we are dealing with a travelogue, this is hardly enough. The characters in *The Wild Bunch* are mere caricatures, whether played by Ernest Borgnine, as he might appear in a dozen other films, or by William Holden, looking serious and dissipated. Robert Ryan may come off best, but that isn't saying much, since he seems deep by being quiet a lot. The slovenly Mexican general is a typical caricature of Mexican generals, as you have seen them in film after silly film. The theme involves a group of desperados who are passé and doomed to extinction in their own bloody game. But there is no depth to the exploration of these characters. There is no substantial comment within the structure of the film to place matters in context. Even so, it *is* possible for a film to make a telling point through a truthful naturalism. *The Wild Bunch* fails dismally here, too, because it glories in its ugliness.

In fact, that is basically the film's only appeal. Peckinpah has sometimes juxtaposed children with the outlaws (employing a touch of symbolism), shown the men looking unhappy in a few scenes, and used extensive slow motion for the killing. Big deal! When it gets down to the guts of the film, virtually every thrust depends upon a killing. The laughs solicited are of the smart-assed variety, generally at the expense of someone else in the movie. One is presumably supposed to marvel at the way the blood spurts on bullet impact, etc. At one point, after someone is shot in the head, the audience laughed at the high-pitched voice of a little boy in the theatre exclaiming: "I like this picture." It is the kind of film that makes many grown-ups behave the same way. Perhaps we have become so conditioned to violence that we delight in the audacity of a film that piles it on with such gusto.

Some prefer it both ways, and attach artistic attributes to the brutality. But because the entire approach to the subject is so banal, even the killing has a curious detachment about it. You cannot feel for anyone. It is a shoot-'em-up, only bloodier, and despite the technical striving for realism, the results are devoid of feeling. My repulsion is more in response to the deriving of entertainment from killing rather than horror at specific atrocities.

I think I understand why some viewers and critics latch on to a film like this. Many intellectuals may be more absorbed in form than content. More

importantly, there is a preference for discovering meaning on their own terms. The self-styled sophisticate often recoils at a film in which a director clearly is attempting to make some social comment. Almost automatically, they eye the film suspiciously and frequently call it heavy-handed. While others may be deeply moved, some tend to see such works as self-conscious. However, a nihilistic movie permits the "discovery" of unapparent meaning and beauty, even in mass slaughter. In varying degrees, I think, such factors are at work in this elevation to discussion level of such nothing-films as Peckinpah's latest.

It is as futile for me to attempt to convince those who dig *The Wild Bunch* that they are wrong as it is for someone to try to sell me on the film's value. However, I think it is appropriate to argue for some kind of re-examination of the relationship of human values to art. Certainly violence and other horrors have their place in movies. The killings in *Bonnie and Clyde* were necessary to illuminate a subject. The cop shot in the face was a horrible sight, as was the demise of the gang. But the violence was meaningful in a context of larger drama. We could hardly enjoy it.

When people begin talking about violence having a beauty of its own, it is logical to consider other cinematic possibilities. What about affecting scenes of true beauty in a Nazi extermination chamber? Or showing the grace of a lynching? Or perhaps the awesome beauty of people being gunned down in an actual riot? I would hope these examples are absurdities. But after some of the reactions to the extensive death scenes in a movie of such shoddy substance as *The Wild Bunch*, I am beginning to wonder and worry.

A Scene from "Doc"

Pete Hamill

[Probably the supreme example of the new trends in anti-Westerns is the destruction of standard heroic figures. The noble Westerner whom Robert Warshow wrote about has become the villain of the revisionist epics. New York newspaperman, Pete Hamill, and director, Frank Perry, tried to create a definitive anti-Western with their 1971 film, *Doc.* This was a retelling of the Wyatt Earp–Doc Holliday relationship and their famous confrontation with the Clanton gang at Tombstone's OK Corral. This story has been the subject of many Westerns—*Frontier Marshall, My Darling Clementine, Gunfight at OK Corral, Day of the Gun*—but in *Doc* all of the old heroes are replaced by cynical opportunists. The sequence reprinted here from Pete Hamill's screenplay illustrates the changing attitude toward the traditional Western morality play.

It should be noted that *Doc* was a critical failure when released and that its calculated cynicism did not meet with audience approval.]

Int: Alhambra [Saloon] —Day

Doc [Holliday] is asleep at a table. His arm is stretched out and his head is resting on it. He has a stubble of beard and looks whiskey-soaked. The place is empty, except for Bartlett who is behind the bar, cleaning glasses. There is a bottle in front of Doc, about two-thirds gone, and a dirty glass.

Wyatt [Earp] comes in the door, carefully, apprehensive. The bar is grey in the muted morning light. Bartlett doesn't look up. Wyatt's footsteps make the only sound. He looks at Bartlett, then at Doc who remains asleep in the far corner of the bar.

WYATT: "How long's he been here?"

BARTLETT: "Last night."

WYATT: "Eat?"

BARTLETT: "Not a bite."

Wyatt walks quietly over to Doc. He lifts the bottle and the dirty glass, and returns to the bar, sliding both a foot towards Bartlett.

WYATT: "How many is this?"

BARTLETT: "Number four."

WYATT: "It's a goddam shame."

BARTLETT: "He's got a right, marshal. He works hard. He runs an honest game. And he's got . . . that sickness. He's got a right to break out every once in a while."

WYATT: "You don't understand . . ."

He walks back to Doc's table, and stands above him.

WYATT: (grim) "John . . ."

Doc's eyes open, but he doesn't move his head. The eyes seem bright and clear, despite the drink-soaked face. Doc sits up slowly, and stares at Wyatt.

DOC: "Buenas dias, Senor muerte."

WYATT: "You look disgusting, John."

DOC: "Oh? Do I? Disgusting?"

Doc stands, rubbing his face. He shivers in the chill of the hangover. He ignores Wyatt and crosses to the bar. He reclaims the bottle of whiskey.

DOC: (to Bartlett) "A clean glass, sir."

BARTLETT: "Sure, Doc."

Wyatt remains standing beside Doc's table, his back leaning against the wall. Doc returns, places the bottle on the table. Then Doc sits down.

DOC: (pouring a drink and not looking up at Wyatt) "What do you want, Wyatt?"

WYATT: "An explanation . . ."

Doc sips the whiskey. He remains silent.

WYATT: "Why'd you bail out the kid?"

DOC: (after a pause, then looking at Wyatt, as Wyatt slides into the chair opposite) "Because I felt like it, Wyatt."

WYATT: "Feelin' that way caused a lot of trouble."

DOC: "What kind of trouble? The kid will be back when Judge Spicer comes through."

WYATT: "Trouble with the Clantons. In jail, that kid was worth something. Especially when it comes to getting to the bottom of that Wells Fargo job. On the outside, he doesn't do me any good."

DOC: "Trouble with the Clantons is your trouble, not mine."

WYATT: "We could have nailed Ringo."

DOC: (emphatically) "Your trouble, Wyatt."

WYATT: "We're gonna have to kill the Clantons, John."

Doc begins to rise. Bartlett steps outside, not wanting to hear.

DOC: "For what? Because Ike Clanton whipped your ass? Because they're 'bad

From the motion picture **Doc.** Courtesy of United Artists 16.

people'? Because you don't like them?" (a pause, as Doc grips the table and leans close to Wyatt's face) "Or is it because it's *you* that's dried up inside, Wyatt, *you* who wants so much to be sheriff that you'll kill for it?"

Doc is wound up, his face bitter. He starts to cough, and moves away from Wyatt, and takes a long drink.

WYATT: (coldly) "I've wanted to say this for a long time, John." (pause) "Something very bad has happened to you. Your sickness, maybe it's gone to your head. Or to your nerve. You ain't the man you were in Dodge."

Doc stands again, and he is laughing under his breath.

DOC: "Tombstone isn't Dodge, Wyatt. Dodge is over. Behind us. As dead as all those poor suckers in Boot Hill. Time is passing us, Wyatt, and you better begin to know what that means. You don't stay twenty-five forever ..."

WYATT: (interrupting) "That woman of yours: she changed you, John. You're not Doc Holliday anymore. I don't know *who* you are."

DOC: "You don't understand, do you? What I'm saying, Wyatt, is that men like us don't mean anything anymore. The railroad's coming. The Federal government is coming. The ranchers and the farmers are coming. The towns are filling up with people who plan to stay. They'll have churches and schools and libraries and music and paintings. This is the last stop, Wyatt. After here, there's only California, and that's already settled. Believe me. I saw it happen in Dodge. You never stayed around long enough to see it happen, but I did. People came to stay for the long haul, and people like us were looked upon as freaks, as rare as buffalo. It's easy now in Tombstone, pulling silver out of the earth. But there isn't enough silver in any mountain to last forever. One morning the silver will be gone and the people will go with it and the houses and the saloons will lie empty, with no companions but the rats and the wind, while the rain washes the adobe back into the earth . . . And then where do we go, Wyatt? Where do people like us go?

WYATT: (after pause, trying dimly to take in the long tirade from Doc) "You're talkin' foolish, John."

DOC: "Maybe I am. But I know this: I'm sick of killing. I'm sick of seeing kids gun down old men to prove something about their manhood. I'm sick of seeing people shot down for bullshit reasons, Wyatt, and I'm sick of shooting them down myself." (a pause) "I'm sick of blood."

Doc is building now, into a kind of frenzy, made up of too much drinking, of frayed nerves, of gnawing remorse, and an understanding of another kind of life.

DOC: "I don't *want* that anymore, Wyatt. I want laughter, and long noisy evenings, and mountain streams, and the sky at morning. I want the sea of grass stretching to the mountains, green and virginal. I want to see winter light hitting the snow at the crest of hills. I want that, Wyatt. I want all of it. Women, dirt, children, laughter, music, wine, mornings, night, smells, sun, water. *All* of it! I want *all* of it. I want to . . . (and then suddenly Doc's voice breaks, from the loudest pitch, to the lowest hoarse whisper) . . . live."

Doc has run down, stunned by his own words. The place is deadly silent. He drops his glass, which splinters loudly. The horror is in Doc's face now, the horror of a man who managed to live past his time by accepting death, the horror of a man who had never allowed himself the luxury of dreaming about a future. He coughs slightly. And then he turns very, very slowly, almost in slow-motion, and starts moving toward the door and the bright rectangle of hard sunlight, moving sluggishly, like a man in a dream fighting off drowning. Then he is gone.

Wyatt is sitting very still. And then, very slowly, he begins to smile, and then to chuckle crazily, and then to laugh, as his triumph floods through him, and we realize, for the first time completely, that Wyatt is the most evil man in Tombstone.

from Indians

Arthur Kopit

[Arthur Kopit's stage play *Indians* has yet to be made into a film. However, it is a highly regarded example of the revisionist genre, as it seeks to arouse the conscience of its audience against the sins of the American past.]

The Indians cover the center area with the huge white sheet, then lie down upon it in piles.

Enter Colonel Forsyth, a Lieutenant, and two Reporters, their coat collars turned up for the wind. Cody is with them; he carries a satchel.

FIRST REPORTER: "Fine time of year you men picked for this thing."

COLONEL FORSYTH: "They're heathens; they don't celebrate Christmas."

FIRST REPORTER: "I don't mean the date, I mean the weather."

COLONEL: "Uncomfortable?"

FIRST REPORTER: "Aren't you?"

COLONEL: "One gets used to it."

SECOND REPORTER: "Colonel, I gather we lost twenty-nine men, thirty-three wounded. How many Indians were killed?"

COLONEL: "We wiped them out."

SECOND REPORTER: "Yes, I know. But how many *is* that?"

COLONEL: "We haven't counted."

LIEUTENANT: "The snow has made it difficult. It started falling right after the battle. The bodies were covered almost at once. By night they were frozen."

COLONEL: "We more than made up for Custer, though, I can tell you that."

SECOND REPORTER: "But Custer was killed fifteen years ago!"

COLONEL: "So what?"

LIEUTENANT: "If there are no more questions, we'll take you to—"

FIRST REPORTER: "I have one! Colonel Forsyth, some people are referring to your victory yesterday as a massacre. How do you feel about that?"

COLONEL: "One can always find someone who'll call an overwhelming victory a massacre. I suppose they'd prefer it if we'd let more of our own boys get shot!"

FIRST REPORTER: "Then you don't think the step you took was harsh?"

COLONEL: "Of course it was harsh. And I don't like it any more than you. But had we shirked our responsibility, skirmishes would have gone on for years, costing our country millions, as well as untold lives. Of course innocent people have been killed. In war they always are. And of course our hearts go out to the innocent victims of this. But war is not a game. It's tough. And demands tough decisions. In the long run I believe what happened here at this reservation yesterday will be justified."

FIRST REPORTER: "Are you implying that the Indian Wars are finally over?"

COLONEL: "Yes, I believe they're finally over. This ludicrous buffalo religion of Sitting Bull's people was their last straw."

SECOND REPORTER: "And now?"

COLONEL: "The difficult job of rehabilitating begins. But that's more up General Howard's line."

LIEUTENANT: "Why don't we go and talk with him? He's in the temporary barracks."

COLONEL: "He can tell you about our future plans." (They start to leave.)

BUFFALO BILL: "You said you'd—"

LIEUTENANT: "Ah, yes, it's that one." (He points to a body.)

BUFFALO BILL: "Thank you."

He stays. The others leave; he stares at the grave. Sitting Bull has entered, unnoticed. Buffalo Bill takes a sprig of pine from the satchel and is about to put it on the grave.

SITTING BULL: "Wrong grave. I'm over here. . . . As you see, the dead can be buried, but not so easily gotten rid of."

BUFFALO BILL: "Why didn't you listen to me? I *warned* you what would happen! Why didn't you *listen?*" (Long silence.)

SITTING BULL: "We had land. . . . You wanted it; you took it. That . . . I understand perfectly. What I cannot understand . . . is why you did all this, *and at the same time* . . . professed your love." (Pause.)

BUFFALO BILL: "Well . . . well, what . . . about *your* mistakes? *Hm?* For, for example: you were very unrealistic . . . about things. For . . . example: did you *really* believe the buffalo would return? *Magically* return?"

SITTING BULL: "It seemed no less likely than Christ's returning, and a great deal more useful. Though when I think of their reception here, I can't see why either would really want to come back."

BUFFALO BILL: "Oh, God. Imagine. For awhile, I actually thought my Wild West Show would *help.* I could give you money. Food. Clothing. And also make people *understand* things . . . better. (He laughs to himself.) "That was my reasoning. Or, anyway, *part* . . ." (Pause.) "of my reasoning."

SITTING BULL: (Slight smile.) "Your show was very popular." (Pause.)

BUFFALO BILL: "We had . . . *fun,* though, you and I." (Pause.) "Didn't we?"

SITTING BULL: "Oh, yes. And that's the terrible thing. We had all surrendered. We were on reservations. We could not fight, or hunt. We could do nothing. Then you came and allowed us to imitate our glory. . . . It was humiliating! For sometimes, we could almost imagine it was *real.*"

BUFFALO BILL: "Guess it wasn't so authentic, was it?" (He laughs slightly to himself.)

SITTING BULL: "How could it have been? You'd have killed all your performers in one afternoon." (Pause.)

BUFFALO BILL: "You know what worried me most? . . . The fear that I might die, in the middle of the arena, with all my . . . makeup on. *That* . . . is what . . . worried me most."

SITTING BULL: "What worried *me* most . . . was something I'd said the year before. Without thinking."

BUFFALO BILL: (Softly.) "What?"

SITTING BULL: "I'd agreed to go onto the reservation. I was standing in front of my tribe, the soldiers leading us into the fort. And as we walked, I turned to my son, who was beside me. 'Now,' I said, 'you will never know what it is to be an Indian, for you will never again have a gun or pony. . . .' Only later did I *realize* what I'd said. These things, the gun and the pony—they came with you. And then I thought, ah, how terrible it would be if we finally owe to the white man not only our destruction, but also our glory. . . . Farewell, Cody. You were my friend. And, indeed, you still are. . . . I never killed you . . . because I *knew it would not matter.*" (He starts to leave.)

BUFFALO BILL: "If only I could have saved your life!"

Sitting Bull stops and stares at him coldly; turns and leaves. Long pause.

BUFFALO BILL: "Well! This is it!" (He forces a weak laugh.) "Naturally, I've been thinking 'bout this moment for quite some time now. As any performer would."

VOICE: "And now to close!"

BUFFALO BILL: "NOT YET! . . . I would . . . first . . . like to . . . say a few words in defense of my country's Indian policy, which seems, in certain circles, to be meeting with considerable disapproval."

He smiles weakly, clears his throat, reaches into his pocket, draws out some notes, and puts on a pair of eyeglasses.

"The—uh—State of Georgia, anxious to solidify its boundaries and acquire certain valuable mineral rights, hitherto held accidentally by the Cherokee Indians, and anxious, furthermore, to end the seemingly inevitable hostilities between its residents and these Indians on the question of land ownership, initiated, last year, the forced removal of the Cherokee nation, resettling them in a lovely and relatively unsettled area west of the Mississippi, known as the Mojave Desert. Given proper irrigation, this spacious place should soon be blooming. Reports that the Cherokees were unhappy at their removal are decidedly untrue. And though many, naturally, died while marching from Georgia to the Mojave Desert, the ones who did, I'm told, were rather ill already, and nothing short of medication could have saved them. Indeed, in all ways, our vast country is speedily being opened for settlement. The shipment of smallpox-infested blankets, sent by the Red Cross to the Mandan Indians, has, I'm pleased to say, worked wonders, and the Mandans are no more. Also, the Government policy of exterminating the buffalo, a policy with which I myself was intimately connected, has practically reached fruition. Almost no buffalo are now left, and soon the Indians will be hungry enough to begin farming in earnest, a step we believe necessary if they are ever to leave their barbaric ways and enter civilization. Indeed, it is for this very reason that we have begun giving rifles to the Indians as part of each treaty with them, for without armaments they could not hope to wage war with us, and the process of civilizing them would be seriously hampered in every way. Another aspect of our benevolent attitude toward these savages is shown by the Government's policy of having its official interpreters translate everything incorrectly when interpreting for the Indians, thereby angering the Indians and forcing them to learn English for themselves. Which, of course, is the first step in civilizing people. I'm reminded here of a story told me by a munitions manufacturer. It seems, by *accident,* he sent a shipment of blank bullets to the Kickapoo Indians, and . . ." (He looks around.) "Well, I won't tell it. It's too involved. I would just like to say that I am sick and tired of these sentimental humanitarians who take no account of the difficulties under which this Government has labored in its efforts to deal fairly with the Indian, nor of the countless lives we have lost and atrocities endured at their savage hands. I quote General Sheridan:—"

The Indians have begun to rise from their graves; for a while they stand in silence behind Buffalo Bill, where they are joined, at intervals, by the rest of the Indian company.

"I do not know how far these so-called humanitarians should be excused on account of their political ignorance; but surely it is the only excuse that can give a shadow of justification for their aiding and abetting such horrid crimes as the Indians have perpetrated on our people."

BUFFALO BILL: "The excuse that the Indian way of life is vastly different from ours, and that what seem like atrocities to us do not to them, does not hold water, I'm afraid!"	*SITTING BULL:* (Very softly.) I am Sitting Bull— (Almost inaudible.)—and I am—*dying!*
"For the truth is, the Indian never had any real title to the soil of this country. We had that title. By *right of discovery!* And all the Indians were, were the *temporary occupants* of the land. They *had* to be vanquished by us! It was, in fact, our *moral obligation!*	*BLACK HAWK:* Black Hawk *is dying.* *TECUMSEH:* Tecumseh *is dying.* *CRAZY HORSE:* Crazy Horse . . . is dying.
"For the earth was given to mankind	*RED CLOUD:* Red Cloud *is dying.*

to support the greatest number of which it is capable; and no tribe or people have a *right* to withhold from the wants of others! For example—"

SPOTTED TAIL: *Spotted Tail . . . is* dying again.

"—in the case of Lone Wolf versus Hitchcock, 1902, the Supreme Court of the United States ruled that the power exists to abrogate the provisions of *any* Indian treaty if the *interests of the country demand!*"

SATANTA: Satanta *is dying.*

KIOKUK: Kiokuk *is dying.*

"Here's another one: in the case of the Seneca Indians versus the Pennsylvania Power Authority, the courts ruled that the Seneca Treaty was invalid since perpetuity was legally a vague phrase. *Vague phrase!* Yes. Ah. Here's one, even better. In the —"

GERONIMO: Geronimo . . . *is dying!*

OLD TAZA: Old Taza *is dying!*

JOHN GRASS: John Grass is dying.

(Long pause.)

"No. Wait. Got it. The one I've been looking for. In the case of Sitting Bull versus Buffalo Bill, the Supreme Court ruled that the *inadvertent* slaughter of . . . buffalo by . . . I'm sorry, I'm . . . reminded here of an amusing story told me by General Custer. You remember him—one o' the great dumbass . . ."

(The Indians begin a soft and mournful moaning.)

(Pause.)

BUFFALO BILL: "Think I'd better close. I . . . just want to say that anyone who thinks we have done something wrong is *wrong!* And that I have here, in this bag, some—"

He goes and picks up his satchel; he looks up and sees the Indians staring at him; he turns quickly away.

"—Indian trinkets. Some . . . examples of their excellent workmanship. Moccasins. Beads. Feathered headdresses for your children."

He has begun to unpack these trinkets and place them, for display, on a small camp stool he has set across the front edge of the center ring.

"Pretty picture postcards. Tiny Navaho dolls. The money from the sale of these few trifling trinkets will go to help them help themselves. Encourage them a bit. You know, *raise their spirits.* . . . Ah! Wait. No, sorry, that's a—uh—buffalo skin."

(He shoves it back in the satchel.)

"Yes. Here it is! Look, just look . . . at this handsome replica of an . . . Indian. Made of genuine wood."

He puts the carved head of an Indian on the camp stool so that it overlooks all the other trinkets. The lights now slowly begin to fade on him; he sits by the trinkets, trembling.

CHIEF JOSEPH: "Tell General Howard I know his heart. I am tired of fighting. Our chiefs have been killed. Looking Glass is dead. The old men are all dead. It is cold and we have no blankets. The children are freezing. My people, some of them, have fled to the hills and have no food or warm clothing. No one knows where they are—perhaps frozen. I want to have time to look for my children and see how many of them I can find. Maybe I shall find them among the dead."

Almost all the lights are now gone; Chief Joseph can hardly be seen; Buffalo Bill is but a shadow. Only the trinkets are clear in a pinspot of light, and that light, too, is fading.

"Hear me, my chiefs. I am tired. My heart is sick and sad. From where the sun now stands, I will fight no more, forever."

And then very slowly, even the light on the trinkets fades. And the stage is completely dark. Then suddenly, all lights blazing! Rodeo ring up. Rodeo music. Enter, on horseback, the Roughriders of the World. They tour the ring triumphantly, then form a line to greet Buffalo Bill, who enters on his white stallion. He tours the ring, a glassy smile on his face. The Roughriders exit. Buffalo Bill alone, on his horse. He waves his big Stetson to the unseen crowd. Then, Indians appear from the shadows outside the ring; they approach him slowly. Lights fade to black. Pause. Lights return to the way they were at the top of the show, when the audience was entering. The three glass cases are back in place. No curtain.

FOR DISCUSSION

1. Critic Pauline Kael maintains in her essays that the Westerns have never been a great American art form or moral reflector of our culture. Compare her criticism of the genre to Robert Warshow's essay in Part III. Do you feel Miss Kael makes a strong case against the Western movie genre? Why or why not?

2. What are some of the typical roles for women in Westerns? Have revisionist film-makers done anything to humanize women in recent Westerns? Is the Western film a totally masculine domain? Can it be made otherwise? How?

3. Are the revisionist Westerns cited as examples in this section an improvement over their counterparts of the past? In what ways are they more realistic and humane (if at all)? How do they reflect the attitudes and concerns of today's generation? Do they tend to create new myths and legends as they work to destroy the old ones? Explain.

Filmography

Filmography

Corral. 12 minutes. Black and white. National Film Board of Canada Production, 1954. Purchase or rental from Contemporary-McGraw-Hill Films.

The Western Hero. 28 minutes. Black and white. CBS TV *20th Century* series, 1965. Check local libraries for loan.

She Wore a Yellow Ribbon. 103 minutes. Color. Directed by John Ford, 1947. Rental from Audio-Brandon Films.

The Left-Handed Gun. 102 minutes. Black and white. Directed by Arthur Penn, 1957. Rental from Audio-Brandon Films.

Ride the High Country. 94 minutes. Color (cinemascope print available). Directed by Sam Peckinpah, 1962. Rental from Films Inc.

Lonely Are the Brave. 107 minutes. Black and white. Directed by David Miller, 1962. Rental from Universal 16.

The Indian

Arrowhead. 105 minutes. Color. Directed by Charles Marquis Warren, 1953. One of the meanest anti-Indian Westerns ever made, with Jack Palance as a ferocious Apache Chief and Charleton Heston as the White scout who defeats him. Rental from Films Inc.

Broken Arrow. 93 minutes. Color. Directed by Delmer Daves, 1952. A pro-Indian movie based on a well-known book about the noble Apache chief Cochise. Extremely well made and with genuine sympathy for the plight of the Indian. However, the good Indians are portrayed by White actors, Jeff Chandler and Debra Paget, and they sound like New England aristocrats. Only Jay Silverheels (remember Tonto?) as the evil Geronimo represents his people with a speaking part. A teacher could use this to contrast with something like *Arrowhead,* but he must point out how both films stereotype the Indian. Rental from Films Inc.

Cheyenne Autumn. 156 minutes. Color. Directed by John Ford, 1964. Ford, whose earlier films killed off more Indians than the entire Seventh Cavalry, really tried to make amends with this version of Mari Sandoz's novel. The film is well done and highly relevant for today's young people. But those Indians—Ricardo Montalban, Gilbert Roland, Sal Mineo—are worthy of more discussion than all the liberalism of the script. Why don't we have any Indian actors? Rental from Audio-Brandon Films.

Hombre. 111 minutes. Color (cinemascope print available). Directed by Martin Ritt, 1967. Paul Newman as a White Indian in a tough, "new-style" film where the Indian is sympathetically portrayed without the platitudes of *Broken Arrow.* Good dialogue and performances as well as excellent use of old Western photographs in the credits. Still at the end, "Indian" Newman saves the Whites by sacrificing his life. Worthy of discussion for its uniqueness *and* its ultimate capitulation to Western conventions. Rental from Films Inc.

Tell Them Willie Boy Was Here. 98 minutes. Color. Directed by Abraham Polansky, 1969. Excellent study of anti-Indian prejudice in the West based on a true incident. The film uses the pursuit of Willie Boy, an Indian, to expose the values of White society. Its major flaw (standard for films about Indians) is the casting of Katherine Ross as a young squaw. Rental from Universal 16.

They Died With Their Boots On. 140 minutes. Black and white. Directed by Raoul Walsh, 1941. No unit on the Indians and the cavalry could be complete without mentioning this extravagant epic on George Armstrong Custer. Errol Flynn plays Custer in what must be Hollywood's greatest whitewash job of all time. Use the film as direct contrast to the actual facts of the massacre and analyze why it is so thoroughly dishonest. Rental from Films Inc.

The Outlaw

Jesse James. 108 minutes. Black and white. Directed by Henry King, 1939. Or, *The True Story of Jesse James.* 93 minutes. Color. Directed by Nicholas Ray, 1957. Both films gloss over the career of one of the most notorious villains of Western history. Take your pick, Tyrone Power (1939) or Robert Wagner (1957) as poor, misunderstood Jesse. Rental of 1939 version from Museum of Modern Art; 1957 version from Films Inc.

Butch Cassidy and the Sundance Kid. 115 minutes. Color. Directed by George Roy Hill, 1969. Popular, funny movie that updates the outlaw myth and gives its characters human frailties that are quite endearing. An excellent example of today's "hip" version of the outlaw myth. Rental from Films Inc.

The Gunfighter

Shane. 117 minutes. Color. Directed by George Stevens, 1953. A famous film that now seems badly dated. (My students seeing it on television hated it.) The gunfighter legend is given a quietly glamorous, even moralistic treatment. Pioneer families like the ones portrayed here never knew a *Shane*. This could be used effectively to contrast with Giants in the Earth. Rental from Films Inc.

The Gunfighter. 85 minutes. Black and white. Directed by Henry King, 1950. The best film of the genre. A quiet, underplayed treatment of the aging gunfighter trying to reform, but haunted by his past. Its theme has been copied often. Rental from Films Inc.

Warlock. 122 minutes. Color (cinemascope version available). Directed by Edward Dmytryk, 1959. An interesting film about a town that hires several gunfighters (Henry Fonda and Anthony Quinn) to clean it up. When their job is finished, they become the new exploiters of the town. It is unique in that the gunfighters are not portrayed heroically. Rental from Films Inc.

The Plainsman. 113 minutes. Black and white. Directed by Cecil B. DeMille, 1936. The granddaddy of the mythological Western, with Gary Cooper and Jean Arthur as "Wild Bill" Hickock and Calamity Jane. A good activity for a class seeing this would be to have them compare the screen images to those of the real Hickock and Calamity Jane. Rental from Universal 16.

The Lawman

My Darling Clementine. 100 minutes. Black and white. Directed by John Ford, 1946. Wyatt Earp, Doc Holiday, and the lawman myth in a pseudorealistic style. Rental from Museum of Modern Art or Audio-Brandon Films.

Gunfight at OK Corral. 110 minutes. Color. Directed by John Sturges, 1957. More of the Earp-Holiday legend, but played in gaudy style by Burt Lancaster and Kirk Douglas. Typical action Western. Rental from Films Inc

High Noon. 85 minutes. Black and white. Directed by Fred Zinneman, 1952. The best of the genre, it actually portrays the lawman as a human being. He is afraid. Contrary to myths created by Westerns that copy its style, Gary Cooper's famous showdown with the Miller gang is not a fast-draw contest. The film might best be studied in context with the times that produced it— the McCarthyist early 1950s. Writer Carl Foreman had a kind of protest in mind in his script. Rental from Audio-Brandon Films.

"Realistic" Westerns

Hud. 112 minutes. Black and white (cinemascope print available). Directed by Martin Ritt, 1963. Rental from Films Inc.

The Real West. 58 minutes. Black and white. NBC *Project 20* Series (narrated by Gary Cooper), 1959. This should be used to develop the extension of the myth, not as a source of history. Purchase or rental from Contemporary-McGraw-Hill Films.

Will Penny. 100 minutes. Color. Directed by Tom Gries, 1966. A rarity in screen Westerns, a believable hero. Will Penny is aging, illiterate, and lonely. Short on dialogue, the film "feels" like the West of the 1880s. Beautifully photographed. Rental from Films Inc.

The Last Hunt. 108 minutes. Color. Directed by Richard Brooks, 1955. This screen version of Milton Lott's brutal novel of the frontier buffalo hunters retains much of the realism of the book. It is most interesting in its description of the actual killing of buffalo. Rental from Films Inc.

Cowboy. 92 minutes. Color. Directed by Delmer Daves, 1958. An Easterner's memoir (Frank Harris) of the West he visited, filmed with quiet dignity and without stereotyped heroics. With Jack Lemmon and Glenn Ford. Rental from Audio-Brandon Films.

This list could go on endlessly. A suggestion to teachers who want to try this unit, but are severely limited by lack of rental fund, would be to rent *any* Western film they can get their hands on. The same effect could be achieved by renting a grade "D" western with Rod Cameron or Buster Crabbe from a local film distributor. Some local camera shops operate film exchanges specializing in these, and they rent as cheaply as $3.00 per film. Universal 16 has plenty of "cheapie" Westerns at low rental rates. With titles like *The Raiders, Wells Fargo, Star in the Dust,* and *The Cimarron Kid,* how could you go wrong? The myth is as plain as day in any of them.

MAJOR 16-MM FILM RENTAL LIBRARIES

American Radio and Television Commercials Festival. 6 West 57th St., New York, N. Y. 10019. Tel.: (212)593-1900.

Anti-Defamation League of B'Nai Brith. 225 South 15th St., Philadelphia, Penna. 19102. Tel.: (215) PE 5-4267.

Appleton-Century-Crofts Films. 267 West 25th St., New York, N. Y. 10001. Tel.: (212) 675-5330.

Audio-Brandon Films. 34 MacQuesten Parkway So., Mount Vernon, N. Y. 10550. Tel.: (914) 664-5051. *Branches:* 2138 East 7th St., Chicago, Ill. 60649. Tel.: (312) MU 4-2531. 406 Clement St., San Francisco, Calif. 94118. Tel.: (415) SK 2-4800.

AVCO Embassy Pictures Corp. 1301 Avenue of the Americas, New York, N. Y. 10019. Tel.: (212) 956-5500.

Bailey Film Associates. 6509 De Longpre Ave., Hollywood, Calif. 90028. Tel.: (213) 466-4331.

Capital Film Exchange. 309 North 13th St., Philadelphia, Penna. 19107. Tel.: (215) LO 7-2698

Carousel Films. 1501 Broadway, Suite 1503, New York, N.Y. 10036. Tel.: (212) 279-6734

Charlou Productions, Inc. 165 West 46th St., New York, N. Y. 10036. Tel.: (212) 247-3337.

Churchill Films. 662 North Robertson Blvd., Los Angeles, Calif. 90069. Tel.: (213) 657-5110.

Columbia Cinematheque. 711 Fifth Ave., New York, N. Y. 10022. Tel.: (212) 751-7529

Columbia University Center for Mass Communications. 440 West 110th St., New York, N. Y. 10025. Tel.: (212) UN 5-2000

Contemporary-McGraw-Hill Films. 230 West 42nd St., New York, N. Y. Tel.: (212) 971-3333. *Eastern Office:* Princeton Road, Highstown, N. J. 08520. Tel.: (609) 448-1700. *Midwest Office:* 828 Custer Ave., Evanston, Ill. 60202. Tel.: (312) 869-5010. *Western Office:* 1714 Stockton St., San Francisco, Calif. 94133. Tel.: (415) 362-3115.

The Film Center. 915 Twelfth Street, N. W., Washington, D. C. 20005. Tel.: (202) 393-1205.

Films Inc.—9 offices, regionally. 1) 227 Pharr Road, N. E., Atlanta, Ga. 30305. Tel.: (404) 237-0341. (Georgia, Alabama, Florida, Mississippi, North and South Carolina, and Tennessee.) 2) 161 Massachusetts Ave., Boston, Mass. 02115. Tel.: (617) 937-1110. (Massachusetts, Connecticut, Maine; New Hampshire, Rhode Island, and Vermont.) 3) 1414 Dragon St., Dallas, Tex. 75207. Tel.: (214) 741-4071. (Texas, Arkansas, Louisiana, New Mexico, and Oklahoma.) 4) 5625 Hollywood Blvd., Hollywood, Calif. 90028. Tel:. (213) 466-5481. (California, Arizona, Colorado, Nevada, Utah, and Wyoming.) 5) 3501 Queens Blvd., Long Island City, N. Y. Tel.: (212) 937-1110. (New York, New Jersey, Delaware, Maryland, Pennsylvania, Virginia, and Washington, D. C.) 6) 2129 N. E. Broadway, Portland, Oreg. 97232. Tel.: (503) 282-5558. (Oregon, Idaho, Montana, and Washington.) 7) 44 East South Temple, Salt Lake City, Utah. Tel.: (801) 328-8191. (Utah and Idaho.)

8) 3034 Canon St. (Kerr Film Exchange), San Diego, Calif. Tel.: (714) 224-2406. (San Diego Metropolitan Area) 9) 4420 Oakton St., Skokie, Ill. 60076. Tel.: (312) 676-1088 (Skokie), (312) 583-3330 (Chicago). (Illinois, Indiana, Iowa, Kansas, Kentucky, Michigan, Minnesota, Missouri, Nebraska, North and South Dakota, West Virginia, and Ohio.)

Film Makers Cooperative. 175 Lexington Ave., New York, N.Y. 10016. Tel.: (212) 889-3820.

Grove Press Films/Cinema 16. 80 University Place, New York, N. Y. 10003. Tel.: (212) 989-6400.

Hurlock Cine World Film Library. 230 West 41st St., New York, N. Y. 10036. Tel.: (212) 868-0748.

Institutional Cinema Service. 29 East 10th St., New York, N. Y. 10003. Tel.: (212) 673-3990.

International Film Bureau. 332 South Michigan Ave., Chicago, Ill. 60604. Tel.: (312) 427-4545.

International Film Foundation. 475 Fifth Ave., New York, N. Y. 10017. Tel.: (212) 685-4998.

Janus Films. 745 Fifth Ave., New York, N. Y. 10022. Tel.: (212) 753-7100

Learning Corporation of America (Columbia Pictures). 711 Fifth Ave., New York, N. Y. 10022. Tel.: (212) PL 1-4400.

Mass Media Ministries. 2116 North Charles St., Baltimore, Md. 21218. Tel.: (301) 727-3270.

Modern Sound Pictures. 1410 Howard St., Omaha, Neb. 68102. Tel.: (402) 341-8476.

Mogull's Film Exchange. 235 West 46th St., New York, N. Y. 10036. Tel.: (212) PL 7-1414.

Museum of Modern Art, Department of Film Circulating Programs. 11 West 53rd St., New York, N. Y. 10022. Tel.: (212) 245-8900.

NET Film Service. Audio Visual Center, Indiana University, Bloomington, Ind. 47401. Tel.: (812) 337-2103.

National Film Board of Canada. 680 Fifth Ave., Suite 819, New York, N. Y. 10019. Tel.: (212) 586-2400

New York Times—Arno Press. Film Division, 229 West 43rd St., New York, N. Y. 10036. Tel.: (212) 556-1651

Pyramid Films. P. O. Box 1048, Santa Monica, Calif. 90406.

Roa's Films. 1696 North Astor St., Milwaukee, Wisc. 53202. Tel.: (414) 271-0861.

Rogosin Films, Inc. 144 Bleecker St., New York, N. Y. 10012.

Samuel Goldwyn 16 mm. 1041 North Formosa Ave., Hollywood, Calif. 90046 Tel.: (231) 851-7234.

Swank Motion Pictures. 201 South Jefferson Ave., St. Louis, Mo. 63166. Tel.: (314) 531-5100.

Teaching Film Custodians, Inc. 25 West 43rd St., New York, N. Y. 10036. Tel.: (212) OX 5-1640. Film excerpts for lease only.

Trans-World Films. 332 South Michigan Ave., Chicago, Ill. 60604. Tel.: (312) 922-1530.

Twelfth and Oxford Sts. Film-Makers Corp. 1550 North 7th St., Philadelphia, Penna. Tel.: (215) PO 3-2585.

Twyman Films. 329 Salem Ave., Dayton, Ohio 45401. Tel.: (513) 222-4014.
United Artists 16. 729 Seventh Ave., New York, N. Y. 10019. Tel.: (212) 245-6000.
University of California, Extension Media Center. 2223 Fulton St., Berkeley, Calif. 94720. Tel.: (415) 845-6000.
Universal 16. 221 Park Ave. So., New York, N. Y. 10003. Tel.: (212) 777-6600.
Walter Reade 16. 241 East 34th St., New York, N. Y. 10016. Tel.: (212) 683-6300.
Warner Brothers 16. 666 Fifth Ave., New York, N. Y. 10019. Tel.: (212) 246-1000.
Willoughby-Peerless Film Exchange. 115 West 31st St., New York, N. Y. 10017. Tel.: (212) 564-1600, ext. 236.
Zipporah Films. 54 Lewis Wharf, Boston, Mass. 02110. Tel.: (617) 742-6680.